SHARP DARTS

Chamber Plays by 7-ON

Donna Abela
Vanessa Bates
Hilary Bell
Noëlle Janaczewska
Verity Laughton
Ned Manning
Catherine Zimdahl

CURRENCY PRESS
The performing arts publisher

CURRENCY PLAYS

First published in 2021
by Currency Press Pty Ltd,
PO Box 2287, Strawberry Hills, NSW, 2012, Australia
enquiries@currency.com.au
www.currency.com.au

Copyright: Introduction © Lee Lewis, 2021; *Aurora's Lament* and *Stella Started It* © Donna Abela 2021; *That Night We Lost Jenny* and *Small Hard Truths* © Vanessa Bates 2021; *Cheering Up Mother* and *The National Apology Centre* © Hilary Bell 2021; *DesertCityIsland*, *Evelyn* and *Robinson* © Noëlle Janaczewska 2021; *Lone Bird* and *Six O'Clock* © Verity Laughton 2021; *Shootin' The Breeze* and *The Politician* © Ned Manning 2021; *The Family Name* and *HereNowThenThere* © Catherine Zimdahl 2021

COPYING FOR EDUCATIONAL PURPOSES

The Australian *Copyright Act 1968* (Act) allows a maximum of one chapter or 10% of this book, whichever is the greater, to be copied by any educational institution for its educational purposes provided that that educational institution (or the body that administers it) has given a remuneration notice to Copyright Agency (CA) under the Act.
For details of the CA licence for educational institutions contact CA,
11/66 Goulburn Street, Sydney, NSW, 2000; tel: within Australia 1800 066 844 toll free; outside Australia 61 2 9394 7600; fax: 61 2 9394 7601;
email: info@copyright.com.au

COPYING FOR OTHER PURPOSES

Except as permitted under the Act, for example a fair dealing for the purposes of study, research, criticism or review, no part of this book may be reproduced, stored in a retrieval system, or transmitted in any form or by any means without prior written permission. All enquiries should be made to the publisher at the address above.

Any performance or public reading of the plays in *Sharp Darts* is forbidden unless a licence has been received from the author or the author's agent. The purchase of this book in no way gives the purchaser the right to perform the play in public, whether by means of a staged production or a reading. All applications for public performance should be addressed to the author c/- Currency Press at the address above.

Typeset by Integral for Currency Press.
Cover design by Mathias Johansson for Currency Press.

Currency Press acknowledges the Traditional Owners of the Country on which we live and work. We pay our respects to all Aboriginal and Torres Strait Islander Elders, past and present.

Contents

Introduction	
Lee Lewis	iv
SHARP DARTS	
Aurora's Lament	1
Stella Started It	17
Donna Abela	
That Night We Lost Jenny	25
Small Hard Truths	36
Vanessa Bates	
Cheering Up Mother	42
The National Apology Centre	51
Hilary Bell	
DesertCityIsland	58
Evelyn	64
Robinson	70
Noëlle Janaczewska	
Lone Bird	75
Six O'Clock	84
Verity Laughton	
Shootin' The Breeze	89
The Politician	92
Ned Manning	
The Family Name	97
HereNowThenThere	103
Catherine Zimdahl	
Appendices	
Production Notes	111
7-On Projects	114
The Playwrights	116

Introduction

Seven playwrights. Fifteen plays. Short plays, yes, but whole worlds contained in them. Huge windows into the minds and times of seven extraordinary writers for the theatre. 7-ON is the name this group uses when they write together. I met them as a group when I was an emerging director working under the mentorship of Nick Marchand at Griffin Theatre Company. It was 2006, I had just graduated from NIDA and Nick was trying an experiment at Griffin of staging short plays before the main advertised play. I knew them as 7-ON before I got to know and love them as individual playwrights. Since first contact I have stayed in a creative relationship with them together and separately and have marvelled at both their individual talents and the creative generosity they give to one another as a collective. This is the group of playwrights who taught me about the value of a community for writers.

There is very little opportunity for critical dialogue in the playwriting world in Australia today. These playwrights talk to one another. Writing is lonely. This group has fought to make it less so. Opportunities for commission and production are increasingly rare. This group celebrates each other's success. In writing together, they have refined their individual voices and challenged each other to move into ideas that none of them would have tackled alone. I do not know the particulars of how and why they formed 7-ON, but I have enjoyed the writing that has sprung from their collaboration.

The short play is so often treated as a theatre problem … what do we do with them? How do we advertise them? Can we add them together in a program of short plays? In this moment of publication I do not have to solve any of those problems. I can simply enjoy the pleasure of their creative visions and appreciate the display of a breadth of capacity that is barely seen on our limited stages. I can enjoy them in the same way I enjoy collections of short stories for the jewels that they are. In this collection I can tap directly into the courage of Donna Abela, the brutal detail wielded by Vanessa Bates, the elegance and sophisticated ordinary of Hilary Bell, the vivid universe making of Noëlle Janaczewska, the precise grace of Verity Laughton, the dynamic rhythms of Ned Manning's dialogue perfectly capturing people in amber, the epic reach of Catherine Zimdahl. It is a rich collection of virtuosity. These plays distil their talents singularly, and the collection displays their unique legacy.

Sharp Darts as a collection is proof of a hard-won depth in Australian playwriting that has provided the foundation for the emerging post-colonial generation. These plays should point you towards the great bodies of work that sit behind each one—these playwrights take up significant space on the Australian play bookshelves. Maybe the collection is your introduction to these playwrights, maybe it will serve as a reminder of their full-length works.

I know that in reading *Aurora's Lament* and *Stella Started It*, the impulse to read Donna Abela's *Jump for Jordan* again is strong. Across her career, Donna has given voice to complex women managing to live in a dominant, often violent, patriarchy. She has always carved space for minority voices in a theatrical landscape which has always been dominantly white. Her politics have been ahead of her theatrical time but her plays are proof that our playwrights have been writing important stories our mainstream theatres have failed to produce.

Vanessa Bates' *That Night We Lost Jenny* is a play that has been timely for too long. The thread of violence in women's lives that is present in the writing of all these playwrights is foregrounded in this work. Vanessa is one of the great writers who has always detailed the aggressions women face and the micro ways that macro problems manifest in the words and rhythms of day to day denial and erasure. There are times though in her writing when she leaps from the real into wilder imaginative spaces and her love story between two gnomes in *Small Hard Truths* is emblematic of that capacity. It's delightful.

You can never get ahead of Hilary Bell's imagination. She often starts in light places but throughout her career she has been willing to explore great darknesses in people and the times. She is expert in wielding the tension of gradual realisation and you can feel her enjoyment of constructing the rising 'On no! Oh no!' in the audience. She loves toying with the way we underestimate certain people in our society—young women (in *Wolf Lullaby*), old women (here in *Cheering*

Up Mother). Hilary's stiletto-like satire when creating a comedy of manners is what makes *The National Apology Centre* so delightful, but what always amazes me is how she maintains a lightness of touch, even when breaking a man's nose.

Noëlle Janaczewska is one of the most literate and formally courageous playwrights in Australia. Her love of and dexterity with complex language drives a vision of our future in *DesertCityIsland*. This is a play I wish would work its way into a long form because selfishly I would love to direct it. She has a virtuosity that is akin to Berkoff, but obviously without the engine of toxic masculinity. This is the kind of high-end Australian language play that we don't see enough of onstage. Noëlle blends comedy with existential horror in in unique ways and while this is definitely a part of *DesertCityIsland* it is a heartbreaking combination in **Evelyn**. Another play that records the female heritage of economic and social precariousness, the nursery rhyme hiding violence in plain sight is deeply unsettling. And you will never look at knitting needles the same way again. For all her aloneness on her island of literature, Jackie is at least physically safer than Evelyn ever was in *Robinson*.

One of the hardest and most rewarding writers to appreciate in this collection is Verity Laughton. Her texts are deceptively simple but the questions they raise are complex. She plays with fluidity and repetition in her structures so that her plays are woven like pieces of fabric rather than linear like string. *Lone Bird* echoes the ancients and the surrealists, giving us a river, a ferryman, the dissolving of memory and identity and hopefully peace. The final word 'water' sends me towards David Foster Wallace's *This is Water*, but it also sends me back to her luminous play *The Sweetest Thing*, which Sarah Goodes directed at Belvoir many years ago. The depth of her writing means that the memories stay with you a long time. *Six O'Clock* has a music in it as she again plays with memory and sadness and love and time … a little reminiscent of Slessor? Or maybe that echo is just because of the period she is evoking.

Ned Manning catches the rhythms of people in such vital ways that they spring up off the page and into the bodies of actors without hesitation. He captures voices of a past Australia that is slipping away from us in *Shootin' The Breeze*: the go-nowhere sounds of a yarn over the fence type conversation are vivid and bring a smile of remembering my grandmother. His devastating cynicism, that speaks volumes about his disillusionment with the politicians of this age, slams home in the final line of *The Politician*. Awful and funny and so true and so sad. In one line. Magic.

There was no way to avoid working through these plays one by one—I am not a writer, just a very grateful director. 7-ON are always listed alphabetically, which thus brings me to the deeply confronting works by Catherine Zimdahl. The portrait of an Australia that refuses to become post-colonial in *The Family Name* is honest and brutal and awful. And then she turns her talent to a world gaze and a style reminiscent of Jose Rivera. In *HERENOWTHENTHERE* she captures the vulnerability of those who have been shifted around the world by violence and who have found questionable refuge in a place that will not care for them.

Taken together, these plays are not a flattering portrait of Australia. They catalogue shame, denial, violence towards women, the burial of colonial violence … all our crimes as a nation. But they reveal that there have always been playwrights prepared to write the dark even when there have not been companies willing to stage these voices. That they do all this in such different and surprising ways is testament to their talent as a group and their generosity as people in embracing their differences. There may not be a national community of playwrights, but through the work of 7-ON you can glimpse our playwriting vision of our nation. The politics are bleak but their writing of it is inspiring.

Lee Lewis

AURORA'S LAMENT
Donna Abela

Characters:

AURORA, *migrant from the Philippines*

LUKE, *young working-class man*

JOAN, *Luke's mother*

TRUCKIE, *truck driver*

Set in a suburban house and street, an office block roof top, a windy south coast caravan park, a highway.

AURORA's *scenes are in the present. To emphasise her sense of isolation and exile, I suggest that only present tense sounds from the caravan park accompany her speeches.* LUKE *and* JOAN's *scenes are all in the past.*

Aurora's Lament *was written for audio. It could, however, also be staged.*

This work is a free adaptation of the Old English poem The Wife's Lament.

PROLOGUE

FX Interior. Caravan in a gale force wind.

AURORA: after weeks of oblique glancing
   fitful sleep
   daydreaming maybes
   we
   between floors
   stairwell sex
   two office block cash-in-hand cleaners
   buckets spilt

rubber gloves off
reaching
touching
going up in the world

    FX Exterior. Office block roof top. Street sounds from below.

LUKE: who knew we had keys to the roof?

with you
heights up here don't scare me!
I'm steady
and I can see all the Sydney bridges
lit up all around us

with you
I can feel my heart plunge and play

without you
I'd know none of this!

    FX Interior. Caravan in a gale force wind.

AURORA: you took me home
took me in
opened up your musty bedroom
and asked about my past

asked enough to know to
leave it be

just sleep-fall with me into a tired tangle
a shared breath
letting your bed
safe as houses
float us away

    FX Exterior. Backyard. Magpies and lorikeets chirp.

LUKE: she lives in the city
with some nuns

near their convent
in a special house for just ladies
is Catholic like us
but she can't stay there forever

she cooks real good
is heaps kind
saves all her pay almost
but she isn't stingy
she brings late night cakes to work
evening tea she calls it
and never lets me pay

she's from the Philippines
her name's Aurora
you'll really like her mum

    FX Interior. A kettle comes to the boil and screams.

JOAN: Aurora
Luke's gone
he left
didn't say why
well before dawn
didn't you hear him getting up?
getting dressed?
forgetting his phone?

dead to the world were you?

well I heard him

did something happen between you two?

It's just that
when Luke stopped doing drugs
he stopped sneaking off
but he's good now
he's got you now

got no reason in the world
has he
to shoot through like this?

 FX Interior. Caravan in a gale force wind.

AURORA: now
in a caravan park
in a grove of grief
on a coast I don't know

I want your olive skin
your chiselled lips under my fingertips

not this punctured heart heaving

Why was I exiled?
What did I do?

 FX Interior. Caravan in a gale force wind. The windows rattle.

PART ONE

FX Interior. A burst of insect spray. A fly being a right pest.

FX Interior. JOAN, *in flip-flopping thongs, barges into the bedroom, spraying.*

JOAN: no Aurora
we don't go back to bed
we get up and get on with it

come on
we'll go for a drive
down south
see Australia
see some of the country
crystal clear coast
blow your mind it will
there's dolphins and that
and shops

fish and fat chips
postcards for your people

come on now
grab some things
got a hat?
do us good
us girls
to get out of the house

> *FX Interior.* JOAN *yanks up venetian blinds. One last spray. The fly dies.*

JOAN: okay?

> *FX Interior.* JOAN, *in flip-flopping thongs, shuffles out and down the hall.*

> *FX Interior. Caravan in a gale force wind. The windows rattle.*

AURORA: I rolled over
but your warm length wasn't there
just the cold shock of sheets
imprinting the ghost of our last moment

I soaked into your pillow
sucked up every last Luke iota

then

friendless

fell off a precipice

> *FX Pause.*

> *FX Exterior. Backyard. Kids next door play cricket.*

LUKE: you've been through too much
but from here on in
I'll catch you

I never felt strong for anyone before
you've made me find more of me
more of me I like
and want to give
if that's okay
to you
with both hands

> *FX Exterior. A kid hits a six. Cheers.*

> *FX Interior. A kettle comes to the boil and screams.*

> *FX Interior. A vacuum cleaner starts up.*

> *FX Interior.* JOAN, *in flip-flopping things, barges into the bedroom, vacuuming.*

JOAN: Aurora
get up
get a move on
come on

I've packed some snags
bacon and eggs and bread
and Bermagui's just got to be seen
it really has
all that
that water

come on
you're not in no convent now
and I'm doing my best
you know
to cheer you up
while Luke's
I don't know
seeing a man about a dog
so no moping on my watch
let's go
a day out

down south
stay the night maybe
why not?
don't you worry

> *FX Interior. Something gets stuck in the vacuum. It shrieks.*

> *FX Interior. Caravan in a gale force wind. The windows rattle.*

AURORA: with no need
no reason
no parting kiss
you took your tenderness
your pledge
and left me with your mother!

> *FX Interior. Caravan in a gale force wind. The windows rattle. The door creaks and bangs.*

> *FX Exterior. Office block roof top. Street sounds from below.*

LUKE: It's just been me and mum
she'll love you but
having a girl in the house
a good influence

I mean
there's no wrong crowd now
gave 'em the flick

chucking sickies
getting wasted 'cause I'm bored
not interested

I'm paying my fines off
drinking half as much

and bringing home someone I want to be different for
and look after
and one day get a house with
and fill it with kids

FX Interior. A kettle comes to the boil and screams.

FX Interior. Caravan in a gale force wind. The windows rattle. The door creaks and bangs.

AURORA: out the window
    crushing camellias
    I fled
    still dressing
    doing up buttons you undid

    car-bogged grass
    concrete swans
    tipped over toys
    I flew
    searching for the city
    for signs to the convent
    for the nuns who rescued me before

    but after me
    up each mute street
    her car prowled
    until I dropped

    FX Exterior. JOAN'S *car prowls up the street and moves in for the kill.*

JOAN: poor Aurora
    was my English not clear?

    hop in

PART TWO

FX Interior. JOAN'S *car driving down the highway. Badly-tuned radio.*

JOAN: this is a safe country
    it works
    no one blows up buses
    which is a shame
    in a way

cause what we've got
others want

they lob up
people smugglers and their customers
red carpet thanks
then rip off decent people
snare our blokes
con them with sob stories
until the free-loading overseas relatives
get every possible cent

worst of all
boat people have done things

traded babies
burnt churches
prostituted

Luke
you don't know him
he's eye to eye with me on this

> *FX Exterior. A hotted up car overtakes and revs off up the highway.*

> *FX Interior. Caravan in a gale force wind. The windows rattle. The door creaks and bangs. A frog croaks.*

AURORA: it started with cake and caution
borrowing mops
holding the lift
polishing the same pane of glass
meeting in the middle
you hanging back
awkward
but attentive
not spoiling for a fight
a fast fuck

a horny skank sex whore to punish

after our shifts
you listened

when you knew about the syndicate
how I'd been tricked
you didn't cut and run

I was not what had been done to me

when you said that
a seed was sown in my blood and boned breast
and you
suited me
so

> *FX Exterior. Backyard. A lawn mower. He needs to shout to be heard.*

LUKE: she didn't come by boat!

she flew here
her visa was legal
she was promised work as a receptionist

anyway
the past is past mum
it's over with

and I know
for the first time
I can go places

because of Aurora

we're each other's second chance
she's not one of us
but she's someone I can really be with

and get married to

and that's what we're gonna do
> *FX Interior. Caravan in a gale force wind. The windows rattle. The door creaks and bangs. A frog croaks.*

AURORA: in a caravan park
in a grove of grief
on a coast I don't know

I kill time in this tin crypt
on a battered mattress
watching
through nylon curtains
cigarette burnt
the trees pleading the pelting wind to stop

who else
dumped like a dog
whimpered here
comparing this sack
to the cradles lovers drift in
microcosmed in quilts
daybreak
a six-hour kiss

and wished this envy
was a bomb
she could drop?
> *FX Interior. Caravan in a gale force wind.*

JOAN: aren't caravans cute?
little homes away from home

you've got everything you need
the beach
the bbq area

the shower block's been done up

the tennis court's brand new

it'll be nice out
when the wind dies down
and the stars come out

anyway

fish and chips?
what you reckon?
couple of prawn cutlets?

I won't be long
I'll just zip up the road

put the kettle on Aurora
I'll be back in no time

> *FX Interior.* JOAN *leaves the caravan. The door creaks open and slams shut.*

> *FX Interior. Caravan in a gale force wind. The windows rattle. The door creaks and bangs. Frogs croak. Nocturnal animals rustle about.*

AURORA: she left a letter
your first ever letter to me

the envelope please …

> *FX Interior.* AURORA *tears open an envelope.*

AURORA: Dear Aurrora

spelt wrong

Bermagui is nice
you'll be nice and safe here
here's some money
I'll come for you soon
stay put

it's for the best
Luke

she
someone
typed it
didn't sign it
seal it with a kiss

didn't hear the one instrument we were
tuned anew
break in two

> *FX Exterior.* JOAN'S *car speeding out of the caravan park.*

> *FX Exterior. Office block roof top. Street sounds from below.*

LUKE: Aurora!
dawn's up!
look!

Wind!
Are you listening?
Aurora wakes up a world in me
Nothing'll ever separate us
nothing
only death
'cause a love for her is lit in me always!

> *FX Interior. Caravan in a gale force wind. The windows rattle. The door creaks and bangs. Frogs croak. Nocturnal animals rustle about.*

AURORA: now
in a caravan park
in a grove of grief
on a coast I don't know
I'm feeding your vow to the possums

> *FX Interior. The door creaks open and slams shut as Aurora leaves the caravan. Nocturnal animals scurry out of the way.*

EPILOGUE

FX Exterior. AURORA *walks on gravel through the pelting wind.*

AURORA: these fallen trees tease me
   ripped out
   their disinterred roots
   tempt my bones to crave the earth

   but this wind
   its punch is a comfort
   it beats up my grief
   insists that I
   heart-crushed
   I'm alive
   I exist

   but our love
   our dawn swan dive off an office block
   does it still exist?

   if yes
   then you
   dear Luke
   you'd suffer as I suffer
   gored by my absent touch
   gripping bloodied slivers of memory

   you'd come

   abort my misery
   before
   I decide that
   my expulsion
   it came with your consent
   cowardly

      FX Exterior. AURORA *walks on gravel through the pelting wind towards a highway. A truck passes.*

how shall I bear this?

shall I do what you
someone
instructed
and stay put?

devote myself
graciously
to silent endurance?

become an icon of faithfulness
and unceremoniously
suck it up?

    FX Exterior. Closer now, another truck passes.

your mum did the dirty work

but you

on the day of her cruelty
you got up
hid your thoughts
and left freely
wordlessly
without
face to face
letting me refute a thing

our vow
you walked out on it
then left me
dependent on
another plotting syndicate
I won't handle this hostility with care

    FX Exterior. AURORA *has reached the highway. A semi-trailer puts on its air breaks and comes to a stop by the end of the final speech.*

may you
protector Luke
be wretched

may grief cut out your heart
and fill you up with a tumult of sorrow

may you be beaten by an icy wind
frost-bitten
drenched
banished from all companionship and solace

may you
treacherous Luke
and all false lovers like you
be hated far and wide
and long horribly for those you have wronged

> *FX Exterior. The door of the semi-trailer opens.*

TRUCKIE: Hop in love

> *FX Exterior.* AURORA *climbs into the truck.*

AURORA: Thank you
TRUCKIE: Where you heading?

> *FX Exterior. The truck door shuts. The truck drives off. The wind continues to rage.*

END

STELLA STARTED IT
Donna Abela

Characters: MARGIE, CATHERINE

MARGIE *is at the arrivals gate.* CATHERINE *is on the plane.*

FLYING

MARGIE: Catherine's flying to Sydney!
   For a visit
   and to march at the Scottish festival with her clan
CATHERINE: MacFarlane
MARGIE: Years ago, we married brothers
   four young people
   we worked hard
   had beautiful healthy children
   enough money
CATHERINE: and had no idea of what lay ahead

HOW WE MET THEM

MARGIE: Larry and Frank
   those brown boys up the shops on motor bikes
   people looked
   tsked at their tattoos
   swords and skulls
   odd accents
CATHERINE: They looked them up and down and thought
   dago
   reffo
   bloody Balmain brawler
MARGIE: But we thought
CATHERINE: a dancing man
MARGIE: a dark charmer
CATHERINE: sweep me off my feet!

MARGIE: be reckless with me!
   I was sixteen
   bored stupid at a one-teacher school
   in a class with kindies
   with better fish to fry
   my eye on my brother's new mate
CATHERINE: on a good behaviour bond
MARGIE: partners in crime sounded fine
CATHERINE: but up the duff
MARGIE: yeah
   pretty quickly
   an unwed mum
CATHERINE: worst thing you could be back then
MARGIE: And that inkling that said don't marry him
CATHERINE: you swapped it for his protective temper
   his Sal Mineo neediness
MARGIE: and the fact that he danced up the street when the baby was born
   You were a saint compared to me
CATHERINE: Old fashioned
   hats and gloves in church
   embroidered hankies
   My siblings were much older
   long gone
   My parents were over kids
   so at a parish dance
   to get out of there
   I said yes to the first boy who asked
MARGIE: Catherine was a virgin
CATHERINE: Margie was a mum with the next bun in the oven
MARGIE: She had a white wedding
CATHERINE: She wore black and had no photos taken
MARGIE: You came back from your honeymoon in shock

FLYING

MARGIE: Catherine fled first
   took her boys to Queensland

    escaped without trace
    and took her maiden name back
CATHERINE: MacFarlane
MARGIE: She'll march with her clan at the festival in Sydney
    I'm picking her up
    Six years it's been
    but we kept in touch
    phoned and wrote
CATHERINE: in secret
MARGIE: shared a lot over many years
    Don't you dare cry when you see her!

LARRY AND FRANK

CATHERINE: Larry made you laugh
MARGIE: He got the kids giggling
    was their funny uncle
    had the lighter heart you thought
    dishing out pastizzis
    bouncing about
CATHERINE: manic actually
    that mad edge
    back then
    no name for it
    no pills for it

    My boys did their homework on the floor
    in the bedroom doorways
    'cause one light
    the loungeroom light
    was all we were allowed to turn on
MARGIE: Frank wasn't as mean
    he cried when my eldest left home
    had a soft spot
CATHERINE: but when drunk
MARGIE: he had fierce eyes
    tiger-suspicious
CATHERINE: Larry didn't drink

MARGIE: Frank lived at the pub
   drove home tanked
   turned into the driveway
   headlights
   through the venetians
   crawling across the loungeroom wall
   We'd read the speed
   guess his mood
CATHERINE: Quick and risky meant slobbery singing
   Kris Kristopherson played too loud for hours
MARGIE: but the slow creep
   the fume
   or the park down the road
   just appear at the back door
   scanning the savannah
   probably meant pounce
   a backhander for the sins we'd committed in his head

FLYING

MARGIE: This is Catherine's first trip back
CATHERINE: No one else knows
MARGIE: I don't want to cry
   I'm Mum the strong one who never cries
   Six years it's been
   we were both still married
   Marriage meant
   be strong
   control your emotions
   Don't you dare be weak!

THE SECRET WAR

CATHERINE: They did love us
MARGIE: some holidays early on
   some good times
   they did love us
CATHERINE: But Malta had been bombed to bits

They'd arrived as kids
watched their mother in the backyard scratching her arms until they
bled
watched her die young
leave them with a father who
during school holidays
to keep them out of trouble
on the front verandah
MARGIE: he'd chain them up
CATHERINE: When they hung hunting rifles in the hallway
poisoned pets
took our pay cheques
grabbed knives during a fight
hit us for having affairs we didn't have
what were they really at war with?
MARGIE: We stayed married
Catholics stayed married
CATHERINE: Did you pray?
Pray that God would take him
not violently
or by car accident
or justifiable homicide
but quietly
in his sleep
if it was God's will?
MARGIE: I did
CATHERINE: So did I
Every night

FLYING

MARGIE: Arrival time
I'm weepy
God this
this is new to me
feeling like this
I don't like it
Pull yourself together!

STELLA GOT US SPEAKING

CATHERINE: Les Senstock's wife Stella
MARGIE: we'd all been out for a drive
   popped in on them
   like you did then
CATHERINE: Stella opened the door and
MARGIE: her face
CATHERINE: one side of her face was black
   burnt black
MARGIE: The men went to the shed
   the kids went to the creek
CATHERINE: but Stella told us everything
   about the tea
MARGIE: the boiling tea
   Les had chucked it at her
CATHERINE: She didn't take milk
   and without milk
   Les said her burn was
BOTH: all
   her
   fault
CATHERINE: Larry said nothing in the car
MARGIE: Frank said nothing
CATHERINE: but Stella had started something
MARGIE: We started to admit things
CATHERINE: couldn't ring too often
   they checked the phone bills
   who we'd been talking to
MARGIE: luckily Catherine could sometimes ring from work
   and
   your back injury
CATHERINE: didn't happen at work
   but I claimed it on compo
   faked a fall
MARGIE: was forced to shift the blame
CATHERINE: And the stitches in your forehead that time
MARGIE: I didn't trip in the laundry

I wanted to say
yes doctor
you guessed it
it was my husband
CATHERINE: We'd known
but didn't
knew
but couldn't say
MARGIE: but now we said everything
CATHERINE: sent letters about things that are crimes now
MARGIE: and we started to rebel
CATHERINE: and life got worse

LANDING

MARGIE: She's landed!
I feel weepy again
all the tears I dammed up
should've cried by now
bloody hell
How do I look?
Your best friend's here
Get a grip!

ESCAPE

CATHERINE: Leaving took careful planning
MARGIE: Courage
CATHERINE: Skim the housekeeping
keep a secret bank account
MARGIE: copy photos on the quiet
CATHERINE: call ahead to the refuge people
pack at the last minute
MARGIE: hide his hunting guns
BOTH: and run
CATHERINE: Margie went south when she left
MARGIE: Bombaderry
CATHERINE: was picked up by lesbians

MARGIE: I'd never seen one before
   They had muscles and flat shoes
   chased down shitheads who left wreaths and death threats in the driveway
   tackled them
   sat on them till the cops came
   and took no lip neither from any of us ladies
   who kicked up a fuss or wouldn't get on

ARRIVAL

CATHERINE *comes through the arrivals gate.*

MARGIE: There she is!
   I feel weepy again
   God
   what's happening to me?
CATHERINE: I hold her
MARGIE: I cry
   I can't stop
   The tears just flood out
CATHERINE: Tomorrow with my clan
   MacFarlane
   we'll march through the streets of Sydney
   thrill to the bagpipes
   the sashes and kilts
MARGIE: the men's gorgeous legs
CATHERINE: screaming with laughter like the girls we were
MARGIE: girls who worked hard
CATHERINE: had beautiful healthy children
MARGIE: enough money
BOTH: and no idea

END

THAT NIGHT WE LOST JENNY

Vanessa Bates

Character: A middle-aged WOMAN, *a Jane Phegan type character*

The WOMAN *turns on CD player. The Cure? Duran Duran? Something early to mid-1980s.*

She dances, awkwardly and then stops. She is, after all, a middle-aged woman, no?

WOMAN: Everyone …

Hesitates. Turns off music.

Everyone does salt and pepper squid
these days. It's nice but it's not

Do you remember?
That night …
That night our English teacher took us to see that movie:
If You Love This Planet.
Dr Helen Caldicott? Hiroshima?
Missile proliferation? Nuclear war?
Getting fingered in the back row.
[*Hastily*] Wasn't in the movie, just the cinema.
And
I think it's quite similar to
London, World War Two
young people
going at it
bomb shelters, air raids
Heightened sense of
According to my granny, anyway.
Sound of an air raid siren …
They were like rabbits, she said.
Rabbits at the end of the world.

Do you remember?
That night …
That night we lost Jenny,
We started off
lying in a circle in the centre of the footy field
heads together
staring up.

In that time.
In that place.
In that moment.

Faint scent of mud and clover in our nostrils
bottle of Jim Beam passed hand to hand overhead.
Stars, pinpricked through the sky
like a face full of pus-blocked pores.

In that time.
In that place.
In that moment.

We were young.
Glorious.
The sexy opening group shot of *St Elmo's Fire*,
bright faces and eternal friendships,
layers and legwarmers,
fishnets and floppy fringes,
striding towards our
brilliant adult
life.

Remember?

The night we lost Jenny.
There was me.
and my new boyfriend Will in his musty lusty green trench coat
and lace-up army boots.

Mel and Sandy: Girls with boobs.
Tim, his best friend James and everyone's best friend Richo.
Jenny, soon to be lost. Her boyfriend Carlos. Soon to be ex.
and Tim's older, way-too-cool-for-school sister,
Rochelle.

Rochelle, recently back from art college in Melbourne.
Cool
and thin, eyes rimmed black.
A neat shiny bob cut in a nod to the mod/ska trend that was taking over
and a long plaited rat's tail in a flirty backward glance at the New Romantics.

On the night we lost Jenny,
Rochelle wore a tartan miniskirt
Doc shoes and a black skivvy
and so would we all, months later, following the glowing tail
of her brilliant burning comet.

She was also smoking a fat cigar.
Gave us a drag and laughed as we puffed and choked
like puppies beside her.
You know, it's not a joint, she said, in her dark sexy voice,
and I blushed, not because I thought it was
but because she thought that *I* thought it was.

The last of us was Michael, same school, same bus,
but not the same, not really.
His eagerness to belong made him not belong and yet at the same time he was tolerated because there had to be someone
who came last.
Remember?

In that time.
In that place.
In that moment.

On the night we lost Jenny,
Carlos broke up with her.

It was a small thing, an easy ritual,
people hook up, get together, then
break up like clods of damp, fragrant earth.

What would happen was that the two doing the breaking up would lag a little behind the main group,
and the one about to be dropped would try and make a joke about it and the other one wouldn't laugh
so that they both understood that whatever easy communication had been between them was now gone.

Then the person doing the dropping would say something like …
I think we should break up now,
or …
I don't reckon we should go together anymore,
and there would be a few seconds of gasping, gulping, grabbing for more time …
You're dropped
finished.
And whatever it was between them,
whatever they once had
sweet, innocent, young love
a secret smile, a shared laugh, a finger in the vagina at a darkly informative end of the world movie,

would just drift up into the crisp clean night air
like smoke from a fat cigar that wasn't a joint.

On the night we lost Jenny,
they drifted back,
her and Carlos,
I glanced over my shoulder a few times and could see her,
red hair blowing around her thin unhappy face.

Tim Bowman did the same thing to me the year before,
same group of friends walking awkwardly in front.

I could have dropped Will's hand and gone back to take hers
but I didn't because having a boyfriend in the group meant I was
    meant to be there.
Even Michael didn't go back
because for an hour, for one full night maybe,
he wasn't last

> *Beat*

In that time.
In that place.
In that moment.

We trudge forward, a school of fish or a flock of geese,
drawn towards a warmer better place, with Rochelle in her Doc
    shoes striding centrally forward at the front of the V
and the rest of us fanning out behind.

Our eyes shining
our mouths wide wet Os of Bonne Bell lipgloss and smartarse
    remarks
sound of our laughter fills the night air. Muffles the crying.

Walking by the river now.
Bad people hang out by the river, under the bridge.
Drop outs and drug addicts.
Kids with pimples and yellow teeth.
They smoke dope. They smash things. They shout abuse and scare
    girls.

These are not the clever people,
the witty people,
the young people who plan to go to university
or art college, or drama school, or America
or even the nearest city, twenty minutes' drive south, and take over
    the world with their clever witty arty dramatic youth.

These are the others.
The other kids.
The ones that sit up the top of the buses, at the back.
When they ever actually bothered to go to school.

The geese pull in tighter around Rochelle, and James and Tim flank her protectively.
If she's nervous it doesn't show
and when a lank haired, string armed man-teen on the riverbank sneers at her, from above the bubbling orchy bottle he holds, in one grimy hand,
she just looks at him, cool, self-knowing
intensely confident, and he falls silent,
dips his baby-fluffed lips into the mouth of his bong
inhales viciously.

Twenty metres upriver
he calls out in a thin reedy voice:
Ya bunch a' sluts,
but we laugh till the tears come
he's quiet once more.

On the night we lost Jenny
it's Michael who notices first.
Michael says: *has anyone seen Jenny?*

Totally dark now
lamps along the main street glowing orange.
And we realize
No-one's seen Jenny for a while.

What about you Carlos? asks Sandy, indignant now,
Mel and I beside her, hands on hips,
eyes glaring.
Any idea what danger lurks here?
In this place, in this moment?
A girl alone, in the dark, by the river ...
She's your girlfriend!

Ex-girlfriend
I broke up with her,
Carlos huffs.
You knew that. I told you I was going to do it.

Whoa.
Wha?
You did?
Who knew?
Who cared?
Side of the road,
squabbling, flapping like crows
turning on each other now.
Blame like a sharp beak peck-peck-pecking

until Mel turns to the obvious culprit.
Michael! What about you? Why didn't you talk to her? You talk to everyone.

Michael's head cranes to and fro

It's not like anyone was talking to you.
You could at least have talked to Jenny.

Michael stutters,
not fast enough, to avoid the storm:

You're a bastard Michael!
She was crying Michael, don't you have any feelings at all?
If she's raped Michael, we know whose fault it is!

His mouth opening and closing like a goldfish.
He tries again:
But I was the one who noticed she was missing.
So?!

A scream!
breaks the night/breaks your heart

wheel around, horrified, terrified at what might be
might already have
happened.

Look!
James points and we see a figure on the other side of the oval, past the far streetlight.
Jenny. Screaming.

And we run.

Tim, James, Carlos and Richard run down the street towards her.
Will, Rochelle and I cut across the oval.
Sandy, Mel and Michael running along the footpath.
No calls for help, to Dad, to police, to mates in cars to fix it for us.
No tweets of alarm or Facebook alerts or YouTube evidence.
No mobiles. Just us.
Remember? Just us.
And
a part of me loves
that I'm running fast
with Rochelle Bowman on one side,
and my boyfriend, Capital B, on the other.

BLAM.
Three of us hit the wire fence at the same time.
Waist high, caught in the gut with a whomp,
thrown backwards onto the grass.

And for a moment we stare up the night sky, gasping, winded.
All those fucking stars.
Then we're up again, climbing over wire, running to the girl under the lightpost, screaming her heart out.

And we reach her at the same time
and she falls sobbing into all of our arms.
Except Michael who holds the tissues.

But what happened?

There was a car …
… and some guys …
and they talked to me and were nice to me … .
… and they offered me a ride in their panel van …

Did they hurt you? Give you drugs?
No, yes, no, yes ... something about pills, something about boys, more screaming.
Sandy and Mel quickly gather, cradle her in a protective circle of jutting breasts and jasmine scented Impulse.

There's a police car over there.

Michael spots it under the yellow lights, no siren or lights flashing, just cruising, curious at the knot of teenagers gathered by the side of the oval.

We should go,
and so we turn and walk again.

We don't think she's telling the truth.
None of us saw a car drive away.
We think she's lying.

I hear the muttering from the others

We think she's lying.

I look at Jenny, smiling bravely, back in the bosom of the group.

We think she's lying. We think she's lying. We think she's lying.
    Beat.
Tonight.
years later,
Carlos (interstate) and Mel (overseas) briefly back in town,

clarion call of text messaging
gathered at that pub up the road ...
reunion. Sort of. Some of us.
Sit round a distressed pine board table with flatteringly darkened lights
muse over growing up in The Eighties.
sing the songs, recall the movies
order another round of drinks.

Look at us, we laugh,
older, fatter, with kids (or not)
mortgages (or not)
jobs that didn't take over the world after all (if we had jobs at all),
alcoholics and addicts and public servants.
No-one ever did go to America. Most didn't make it out of the state.

And then the story of The Night We Lost Jenny comes up.
And this is serious.
We stop laughing, order more drinks and the waiter, half our age, recommends the salt-and pepper-squid.

Over our beer,
crisp white wines,
pub meals and potato wedges,
salt and saturated fat
we talk the night over and over.

Do you remember?
Do you?
The panel van? The pill? The screaming?

Loudly interrogate each other,
lips greasy, red faces,
more wine, more squid.
Someone says he remembers Jenny had always been slightly mad and someone laughs and says she kissed someone else, so Jenny wanted to get back at them.

Someone asks about the joint, perhaps that was the reason, and everyone cracks up again, *it wasn't a joint! Did you think it was a joint? It was a cigar!*

Remember? Remember? *Remember?*
Not really. No.

The only one who actually knows, we decide, as we drain our glasses
lick our fingers, eat our fucking salt and pepper squid, is you, Jenny,
and you're gone.

In that time.
In that place.
In that moment.

It was almost as if, from that night,
you simply drifted further and further from our lives
until finally,
you were lost for good.

Like … the eighties.
Or youth.
Or a rabbit, scared by an air raid siren,
who fell off the end of the world.

END

SMALL HARD TRUTHS

Vanessa Bates

Characters:

JANET, *a female gnome*

KEITH, *a male gnome*

Two smiling gnomes. They stand quite close to each other but face out in different directions. JANET, *modestly dressed in long sleeves and skirt, carries a straw basket.* KEITH *wears a waistcoat and holds out a fishing rod. They both wear large pointed red hats.*

JANET: I spy with my little eye, something beginning with … L.
KEITH: Um … letterbox?
JANET: Yes, your turn.
KEITH: I spy with my little eye, something beginning with B.
JANET: Birdbath?
KEITH: Yep.

> JANET *freezes as she watches a drunken couple stumbling pass.* JANET *has seen them come in but not* KEITH.
>
> *A moment.*

JANET: Oh for fuck's sake. What time do you call this?
KEITH: Sorry?
JANET: I said, what time do you call this? Did you hear those two? I could see them and she was *off her face*.

> *Pause.*

You should have seen what she was wearing. Or rather … not wearing.
KEITH: It's none of our business Janet.
JANET: I didn't say it was our business. I said, did you hear them, just now?
KEITH: I was asleep.

> JANET: Let me paint you a picture. Skirt up round her butt, knickers

down round her ankles. She was sticking her tongue in his ear and grabbing at his crotch. He had his hand up her ass like she was some sort of sex muppet. [*Sniffs*] This whole garden reeks of bourbon. [*A beat*] You were *not* asleep.

    Pause.

You can't sleep, Keith, your eyes are painted open.

KEITH: I was meditating.
JANET: You were not meditating …
KEITH: How would you know? How would you know what I was doing?
JANET: I know you weren't meditating.
KEITH: You don't even face in my direction.
JANET: That is not my fault.
KEITH: Janet, you don't face me, you face the letterbox.
JANET: I don't 'face the letterbox', I face the garden gate, it's meant to be welcoming. It's the way I've been positioned, I can't help the way I've been positioned.
KEITH: Well the last gnome in that position …
JANET: Oh, for fuck's sake Keith are you going to bang on about Sylvia again? I'm sick of hearing about her. Sylvia was sensitive, Sylvia was talented, blah blah blah. She wasn't even a proper gnome, she was a fibreglass weasel.
KEITH: She was a stoat.
JANET: Stoat, weasel, mongoose, rat, who gives a fuck? She was vermin and I'm glad that drunken Australian backpacker managed to crowbar her out.
KEITH: You're just saying that. You don't mean it. He … he stole her.
JANET: Boo hoo. She's probably somewhere on Bondi Beach by now with a clacker full of sand and a can of VB balanced on her head. That was more her style. You forget, I used to sit next to the birdbath. I could see more than enough of Smug Pants Sylvia. And you.
KEITH: You know, Sylvia used to play the piano accordion. She was actually very talented.
JANET: She was *holding* a piano accordion. That's all. She didn't play the thing Keith, she just held it. Just like I hold a basket and you hold a fucking fishing rod. I don't gather daisies and you don't reel in salmon. They're props Keith, that's all they are. Props!
KEITH: She wore a waistcoat. And a little string of pearls.

JANET: But she didn't have a hat, did she? She didn't have a pointy red hat.
KEITH: She didn't have a pointy red hat, no. What's *your* point Janet?
JANET: My point is: she wasn't a proper gnome.
KEITH: You didn't know her like I knew her. Sylvia had ... gnomish sensibilities.
JANET: Whatever.

> *Pause. A sound.* KEITH *and* JANET *immediately display their gnomish smiles.*

> *Footsteps getting close. Loud sound of falling water.* JANET *and* KEITH *look pained.*

FEMALE VOICE: *Are you pissing in my rockery again?*
MALE VOICE: *No. Yes. Maybe.*

> *Footsteps hurrying away. Door opens and closes. Pause.*

KEITH: When did it get like this?
JANET: Do you mean the being pissed on?
KEITH: No. Us. The bickering. The hating. Sometimes I feel like ... we're so far away from each other. I know there's a rockery between us but these past weeks I feel like there's so much more ... Are we growing apart Janet? Is that it?
JANET: We can't grow apart, we've been cemented in.
KEITH: True.
JANET: I think it's good to have some distance. Look at her. And him. How embarrassing. You wouldn't want me falling all over you like that. [*Pause.*] Would you?
KEITH: No, no of course not. We'd probably just ... smash our hats.
JANET: It's ... it's better this way. We've been standing in this garden for a long time now. All that sun and driving rain. I'm not as— vibrant as I once was.
KEITH: Janet ... don't.
JANET: It's true. I'm actually quite faded. I'm almost glad you don't have to face me. I'd rather you remember me as I was. In the birdbath.
KEITH: Remember my eyes Janet. Do you know what colour they're painted?
JANET: I caught a quick glimpse when he was troweling in the cement but ...

KEITH: I thought so.
JANET: They're blue.

> *Pause.*

> Things have changed. I feel life is just passing us by, day in, day out. People don't really want gnomes anymore. They want copper hedgehogs and terracotta Fairies Live Here signs. And and ... fiberglass rodents. I don't know how it happened but we're passé.

KEITH: We are not passé. We're retro.
JANET: I want to get drunk.
KEITH: Janet?
JANET: You heard me. I want to drink bourbon and slur my words and throw my skirt over my hat. I want to grab your crotch and stick my tongue in your ear. I want to be a sex muppet.
KEITH: I've only ever wanted two things. To catch a fish, and to see you face to face Janet. Think of that, face to face. I dream of that moment. Well, meditate.
JANET: [*Touched*] That's ... nicer than being a sex muppet. You're a nice gnome Keith. You always were.
KEITH: Nice gnomes go nowhere. We could turn Janet. If we really wanted to, we could turn.
JANET: But the cement ...
KEITH: Let's try. Let's try for a miracle. You and me. We've got something very strong here, very ... concrete. Am I wrong?
JANET: No, but. We could end up falling on our faces, you realize that?
KEITH: It's worth it Janet.

> *With a herculean effort the two gnomes try to wrench themselves around to face each other. Quite painful.*

JANET: My feet! They're cracking!
KEITH: Use your basket as leverage! Ahhh! My ankles!

> *And with a final cracking sound* KEITH *manages to turn and face* JANET. *Except ... she hasn't turned.*

KEITH: Janet? I've done it Janet! I turned. I can almost see your profile. You can do it too!
JANET: No.
KEITH It's not impossible! Turn Janet, turn.
JANET: No Keith.

KEITH: No?

JANET: I'm not turning. This is where I was positioned.

KEITH: And you can change your position! I'm proof!

JANET: And in the morning when he comes out and pisses on us again, he'll pick you up and turn you round again, to face the birdbath. It's hopeless Keith. You've shattered your ankles for nothing.

KEITH: Not for nothing Janet. I thought you and I … were different. Special. Beyond cement.

JANET: We are gnomes. We are not special. Look, I know you dreamed of some sort of miracle.

KEITH: Meditated.

JANET: Whatever. There are no miracles. Not for the likes of us. It's not me you should be facing Keith. It's reality.

KEITH: Oh Janet …

> *Suddenly,* KEITH'S *rod dips and jerks … he calls to her urgently.*

KEITH: Janet! My eyes are not blue! I have one blue eye and one olive eye!

JANET: And I have lichen and a colony of spiders living in my basket. What's your point Keith?

> *But* KEITH *is unable to answer, he is straining against the line, it suddenly pulls him out of his position on the rockery, he is moving freely about the stage, trying to catch his fish, the rod is quivering and waving, until suddenly he mimes/pulls an enormous fish up out of the non-existent pond. He drops the rod, holding the flapping fish in his outstretched arms. He is grinning, gaping, amazed, alarmed, ecstatic, all at once.* JANET *can't see any of this and keeps rabbiting on.*

Fine, be like that. Sun's nearly up. Another day, just like yesterday. And the one before. Damn this basket's heavy. Keith! Are you crying? Because I'm really getting tired of this whole limp gnome routine. Man up Keith.

> *But* KEITH *is lost for words in the wonder of his big fish. He kisses it tenderly and then drops it back in the pond, waving as it swims away. And for a moment, he too contemplates the concept.*

Did you hear me? Are you ignoring me Keith? Have you got the sulks? Or are you meditating, is that it? Keith? Keith! Keith! Are you there?

And he walks back and takes up his original position.

KEITH: Of course I'm here Janet. Where else could I be? [*Pause*] I spy with my little eye, something beginning with B.

JANET: Um ... birdbath?

KEITH: Yep. Your go.

JANET: I spy with my little eye something beginning with L.

KEITH: Love.

A slight pause. JANET *tenses.*

I'm joking. Letterbox.

JANET: [*relaxing again*] Yes! Letterbox. Your go.

END

CHEERING UP MOTHER
Hilary Bell

Characters: MOTHER, DAUGHTER, SON, CAT

SCENE ONE

MOTHER, SON, DAUGHTER, CAT.
MOTHER *is in a rage.*

SON: Mum, you've been so miserable and grey
　Since poor old Dad, God bless him, passed away—
DAUGHTER: A whole year since we laid him in the ground,
　And *still* you're not much fun to be around.
SON: It pains us both to see you so upset.
DAUGHTER: That's why we thought you might enjoy a pet.
MOTHER: Well you were wrong. The last thing that I need
　Is some foul, meowing, drooling maw to feed!
　Some scrawny Tom to yowl and shred my curtain,
　To drag in chewed-up rats—
DAUGHTER: Mum, keep your shirt on.
MOTHER: To piss among the plants, shit on the stairs,
　To cover all my clothes with orange hairs.
　There's nothing more than cats that I detest.
　Frankly, kids, I'd rather be depressed.
SON: But look how cute he is! He needs a home.
MOTHER: I'm sure he's got some relatives in Rome.
DAUGHTER: Well thanks a lot. Most mothers would be grateful.
MOTHER: For what? You've never done a thing so hateful.
SON: I'm sorry, they won't let us take it back.
MOTHER: Then throw it under an on-coming Mac.
DAUGHTER: You're crazy, any normal mum would love it.
MOTHER: Well any normal mum can go and shove it.
　I hate that cat. Go drown it in a well.

I'm going to church. You three can go to hell.

She storms out.

SON: I guess this means we drive it back to Mudgee.
DAUGHTER: I told you we'd do better with a budgie.
SON: A bird, a fish, she'd still get in a lather.
She misses Dad, she'll never love another.
DAUGHTER: Well no-one's going to love a hag like that,
Not even this revolting yellow cat.
SON: *I* can't take him, now we've got the baby.
DAUGHTER: She's mental, there's no well! The toilet, maybe …
SON: You take him back to uni, in defiance.
DAUGHTER: They'd just end up dissecting him in Science.
SON: So you don't care about him!
DAUGHTER: Nor do you!
SON: Well then, there's only one thing we can do:
Let's leave him here with water and some food
And hope a few Hail Marys change her mood.
DAUGHTER: It's Sunday, so she does the altar flowers.
That cheers her up a bit before she sours.
SON: It's Eucharist—she'll chat with Father Flaherty,
And come home full of Christian love and charity.
DAUGHTER: She'll open the front door and: 'Look at that!
What *was* I thinking? Welcome, darling Cat!'

They run off, leaving the CAT.

MOTHER *enters. She shrieks.*

MOTHER: What? You still here! That pair of steaming turds!
Why not a fish? A couple of lovebirds?
You are not welcome. I don't want you here.
You make me sick. Do I make myself clear?
I cannot bear to touch your mangy coat,
But if I could, I'd grab you by the throat
And hurl you off the top of some skyscraper.
Now go away. I want to read the paper.

She settles in.

CAT *watches, then rubs himself around her legs.*

MOTHER: You are not here. You don't exist. You're dead.
　You won't be patted and you won't be fed.
　You touch my legs, I swear I'll call the police.
　[*Sobs*] Oh God! Why won't you let me grieve in peace?
CAT: If anything could move a heart of stone,
　It is to see a woman weep alone.
　I know your loss and how you suffered then.
　I've heard it said you'll never love again.
　But even when our life seems most monotonous,
　We find, my dear, that Love has not forgotten us.
MOTHER: I beg your pardon?
CAT: I just said—
MOTHER: I heard.
　I'd thank you not to say another word.
　Of course to hear a cat speak is surprising,
　But who'd have thought you'd be so patronising?
CAT: I simply meant—
MOTHER: What's more, I never foller
　Advice from someone wearing a flea-collar.

　　She reads the paper.

CAT: Excuse me—
MOTHER: Oh, for God's sake!
CAT: Be a friend
　And let me have a loan of Good Weekend.
MOTHER: Don't tell me you're a culture-loving pussy.
CAT: I want to sit on it … I like Debussy.

　　CAT *claws at the paper till he's comfortable.*

MOTHER: They think I need a cat now that I'm greying.
　—Don't get too comfortable, who said you're staying?—
　They stick a crochet hook into one fist
　And send old codgers round for games of whist.
　They're doing all they can to antiquate me.
　Why not save time and bloody well cremate me?
CAT: Your comfort, nothing more, was in their sights.
　They sent me to relieve your lonely nights.
MOTHER: I'm lonely! But you cannot, after all,

Replace a husband with an old hairball.
There's some things that a cat can't satisfy.
A cat's a cat, and that's that.
CAT: … I can try.

SCENE TWO

SON, DAUGHTER.

SON *holding baby.*

DAUGHTER: It's great, I haven't heard from her for days!
SON: We have her round for tea—she never stays.
Last week I got a phone call from the church:
She'd left the Sunday Schoolers in the lurch.
DAUGHTER: I needed her to wire me some cash.
She said, 'Buy yourself a nice big piece of hash.'
SON: I ask her would she like to sit for Lizzie.
She used to jump—but now she says she's busy.
DAUGHTER: It's great!
SON: I hope it lasts.
DAUGHTER: And how's the cat?
SON: It's weird, she giggles when I ask her that.

SCENE THREE

MOTHER, CAT.

MOTHER *hurls a bowl of cat food onto the floor.*

MOTHER: That's all you're getting. If you dare complain
I'll make you puke and then eat it again.
CAT: As long as it's prepared by you, the odds
Are that it is the Nectar of the Gods.

    MOTHER *blinks, while* CAT *eats.*

CAT: I'm thankful that you're feeding me at all,
Considering I'm just an 'old hairball'.
Considering at first I had to scrounge
For year-old leftovers behind the lounge.
I'm thankful that as yet you haven't kicked me,

Or carried out your promise to evict me.
Those lonely lanes ... It would have been so shabby
Carousing with some overheated tabby.
MOTHER: What tabby?
CAT: One who'll never come between us.
MOTHER: Well what's her name?
CAT: Her owner calls her Venus.

    MOTHER *throws down more food.*

MOTHER: Don't guzzle, you'll end up with indigestion.
CAT: I s'pose a little pat's out of the question?

SCENE FOUR

SON, DAUGHTER, MOTHER, CAT.

CAT *sits apart. Throughout the scene,* MOTHER *is distracted by him.*

SON: We thought you'd *like* a picnic by the pond.
DAUGHTER: What's in your hair? Don't tell me you've gone blonde!
MOTHER: Of course not. [*To* SON] Well I wouldn't. Not today.
    Look at those clouds.
SON: What clouds?
DAUGHTER: It's blonde!
MOTHER: It's grey!
SON: The kids are yelling for their old grandma.
MOTHER: Poor kiddies.
DAUGHTER: Mum, you ought to wear a bra.
MOTHER: I've stuff to do.
SON: You never do a thing.
MOTHER: Excuse me?
DAUGHTER: Did you *lose* your wedding ring?
SON: You didn't do the flowers for the church.
MOTHER: I miss it once, you lot send out a search!
DAUGHTER: What next? You gunna get a nip-and-tuck?
SON: It hurts to see your mother run amok.
DAUGHTER: There's something going on—you're acting shifty.
SON: Mum don't forget, you *are* approaching fifty.
MOTHER: I'm busy! Off you go.

SON: The kids'll wonder.
MOTHER: Well I don't give a damn!—It's going to thunder,
But you have fun. Now that's the end of that.
DAUGHTER: But Mum—
SON: *Please* Mum—
MOTHER: I have to feed the cat.

SCENE FIVE

MOTHER, CAT.

MOTHER *feeding* CAT.

MOTHER: I'm chopping up the duck all nice and fine.
And here's a bowl of milk!
CAT: I have some wine.
MOTHER: … A glass for that, or will a saucer do?
CAT: A bowl for me, a crystal flute for you.

> MOTHER *astonished as* CAT *reveals an elegantly set table.*
>
> *He lights the candles.*

CAT: How did you do the duck?
MOTHER: With mandarin.
CAT: To eat a duck alone would be a sin.
Sit down and tell me which part you like best—
A little thigh perhaps? …A little breast?

> CAT *serves.*

CAT: You're looking very lovely, Della.
MOTHER: Pardon?
CAT: I so enjoyed our digging up the garden.
MOTHER: You know so much—those earthworms, tree-roots, stones.
I'd not appreciated old fishbones.
CAT: I know a lot, but I would swap it all
For just a smidgen of your childlike thrall.

> *They stare at each other, entranced.*

CAT: Almost forgot!

> CAT *jumps up, putting on music.*

MOTHER: Debussy.
CAT: Care to dance?
   There's nothing beats a nocturne for romance.
   They dance.

SCENE SIX

DAUGHTER, SON.

SON *laden with babies, shopping, briefcase, dry-cleaning.*

DAUGHTER: I knocked and knocked until my knuckles bled.
SON: The phone was off the hook. What if she's dead?
DAUGHTER: I called for money, she said, 'Ring back later'.
SON: She won't sit for the kids, and now they hate her.
DAUGHTER: She wouldn't let me stay there this weekend—
   She said, 'Just for a change, sponge off a friend'.
SON: The church adored her once, they couldn't fault her.
   Now they send nasty notes about the altar.
DAUGHTER: As for the cat we bought her out of pity,
   I'll bet he's met an end that's none too pretty:
   Neglected, starved to death,
SON: Or died of thirst.
DAUGHTER: Prepare yourself, whichever, for the worst.
SON: I say we bash the door down—after three!
   A-one, a-two—
DAUGHTER: Hang on, I've got a key.

   They enter.

SON: Mum?
DAUGHTER: Anybody home?
SON: No sign of her.
DAUGHTER: There's no dead body.
SON: Almost wish there were.
DAUGHTER: I can't make out a thing in all this gloom.
SON: A crack of light! She must be in her room.

   They throw open the door, to reveal CAT *and* MOTHER *in bed, flagrante delicto.*

ALL: ARGHHHHHHH!!!!!!!

> *Everybody runs helter-skelter. The kids pounce*—SON *on* MOTHER, DAUGHTER *on* CAT—*smothering them with pillows.*

DAUGHTER: Revolting!
SON: Perverts!
DAUGHTER: Monsters!
SON: Demons!
DAUGHTER: Freaks!
SON: You're sick.
DAUGHTER: You're mad.
SON: You pair of smutty sneaks!
CAT: Wait—
MOTHER: You don't understand—
CAT / MOTHER: We love each other.
SON: You kill the cat.
DAUGHTER: And you can murder Mother.

> MOTHER *manages to hurl* SON *off but is too late to save the* CAT.
>
> *She wails as* DAUGHTER *holds up his corpse.*

MOTHER: O curs'd Electra, you have killed my King!
DAUGHTER: What—this old scraggy molting orange thing?
MOTHER: O curs'd Orestes—you attempt to smother
   The very life that gave you life: Your mother!
   O God in Heaven, Holy Lord on High
   Look down and hear a mother's anguished cry!
   I charge you to attack him and assault her,
   Or nevermore I'll do your Sunday altar.

> *She crumbles.*

SON: She's lost her mind.
DAUGHTER: I know, but how? And when?
SON: I'll never pat a pussycat again.
DAUGHTER: I'd be struck blind if I could have my wish.
SON: Imagine if we *had* bought her a fish …
DAUGHTER: It's not our fault the cat was warped.
SON: Far from it.
DAUGHTER: To think his—

SON: Don't.
DAUGHTER:—in her—
SON: Stop!
DAUGHTER: Oh, I'll vomit.
SON: From all this filth can any sense be made?
DAUGHTER: I guess the lesson is, you get 'em spayed.

   Celestial music. CAT'S GHOST *appears in dazzling light.*

   MOTHER *is ecstatic as* CAT'S GHOST *lifts her in his arms.*

CAT'S GHOST: Cats get nine lives, but boy the time goes fast!
  And thanks to you, I've just used up my last.
  You curse the so-called crime we're guilty of,
  But you, not we, are Heretics of Love.
  It's you destroy the sweet and noble play
  Of Cat and Woman rolling in the hay.
  It's we who now ascend on Heaven's breeze
  To scratch and yowl and purr just as we please.
MOTHER: Goodbye, you wicked children, and good luck.
  Thanks for the cat, he was an awesome … friend.

   CAT'S GHOST *and* MOTHER *ascend to heaven.*

SON: What will we tell the kids?
DAUGHTER: The church?
SON / DAUGHTER: 'The End.'

END

THE NATIONAL APOLOGY CENTRE
Hilary Bell

Characters: NATALIE, ROBIN, *any gender*

The lobby of a shopping mall.

ROBIN *approaches* NATALIE.

ROBIN: Excuse me, are you Natalie?
NATALIE: … Yes.
ROBIN: I'm here on behalf of Andrew.
NATALIE: Andrew? Is he here?
ROBIN: If I can just have two minutes of your time.
NATALIE: Is he alright? Is everything alright?
ROBIN: Natalie.
 I am aware of your suffering. This past six months has been a very difficult time for you. Quite apart from the emotional toll, there are the many practical difficulties you've encountered. You were obliged to move out of the home you shared with Andrew, and at the age of forty you're living with your parents. Feeling worthless you have let yourself go, putting on weight and resuming your addiction to chewing tobacco. The depression has had a negative impact on your creative output, and I understand that you are now experiencing severe writer's block.

 ROBIN *motions for her not to interrupt.*

These unfortunate facts mar the happiness of the man who was once your husband.
NATALIE: / Sorry, what is this?
ROBIN: / It's been hard for Andrew, seeing someone he used to love in such pain. He acknowledges that he is the cause. Naturally, you want to know why things ended so abruptly.
NATALIE: / Are you a friend of his?

 ROBIN *motions for her not to interrupt.*

ROBIN: / He felt that with his mind already made up, prolonged discussion would be pointless. His priority was to spare you the humiliation of an uncomfortable scene, which is why he took the step of informing you of his decision by text, and then changing the locks.
    Now that six months has passed, he hopes that any inflamed emotions have calmed enough for you to be able to listen to, and accept, his sincere apology.

NATALIE: Who are you?

ROBIN: My name's Robin but that doesn't matter, I'm here representing Andrew.

NATALIE: Did he send you?

ROBIN: Not me personally, but—

NATALIE: What do you want?

ROBIN: It's what Andrew wants, Natalie: to apologise.

NATALIE: I'm really confused.

ROBIN: It's as simple as that.

NATALIE: How did you find me?

ROBIN: Your mother said you'd be here.

NATALIE: Have you been to my house?

ROBIN: She said you come to the mall for the free wifi.

NATALIE: Andrew sent you.

ROBIN: My card.

NATALIE: 'The National Apology Centre'.
    Got it.

ROBIN: So, if you could just sign— Or you can use your finger, either works.

NATALIE: I'm not signing.

ROBIN: There's no charge, it's a gift.

NATALIE: I don't want it.

ROBIN: Are you saying you don't accept his apology?

NATALIE: That's right.

ROBIN: I'm not sure you can do that.

NATALIE: I just did.

ROBIN: Hang on a sec.

NATALIE: Thank you.

ROBIN: No, wait, I'm thinking, I haven't had this hasn't happen before,

I don't know what to do. I'll need to call the company about the protocol. Maybe it's here somewhere ...

ROBIN *scrolls through iPad.*

NATALIE: Thank you, have a good day.
ROBIN: We're engaged to deliver a service.
NATALIE: You've done your job.
ROBIN: But it's unresolved.
NATALIE: Not my problem.
ROBIN: I don't understand, why would you reject it?
NATALIE: I'm not getting into an argument.
ROBIN: It's a nice gesture: he hurt you, he wants to make up for it.
NATALIE: Why are you still here?
ROBIN: I'm new at this, I have to be prepared for all contingencies—please, would you mind explaining?
NATALIE: You don't have some vague idea?
ROBIN: I'd really appreciate it.

Pause.

NATALIE: Imagine I were to punch you in the face.
ROBIN: Yes.
NATALIE: And after the passage of time, a week, I sent somebody along to say sorry. Sorry, for what I did to you.
ROBIN: Hmm. I see.
NATALIE: How would you feel?
ROBIN: I guess it depends.
NATALIE: On what?
ROBIN: How much you spent. If you'd broken my nose and you went for the budget deal then yeah, I'd be pretty upset. Is that the problem? He paid for a mid-range apology. It may not be quite the same as a bespoke one, but it's not cheap.
NATALIE: No.
ROBIN: No?
NATALIE: It's because he sent you.
ROBIN:—
 Oh! Oh ... Well again, if you buy the bespoke package you get somebody more attractive. If you want real top-of-the-range, we

have dignified older gentlemen or beautiful young women, who arrive with a gift-wrapped box of soaps.

NATALIE: He sent a stranger, with a phony speech.

ROBIN: If you mean the speech is too formal, we also offer homestyle.

NATALIE: What?

ROBIN: Homestyle. Basic vocabulary, no elaboration, mutter and avoid eye-contact—

NATALIE: I don't want homestyle, I want Andrew here.

ROBIN: Wouldn't that be very awkward for you both?

NATALIE: Exactly, yes. But worse for him.

ROBIN: I see, so it's spite, you want him to suffer.

NATALIE: I do but that's irrelevant. The point is, what the hell kind of an apology is it if it's made by someone else?

ROBIN: A clean and painless one.

NATALIE: For him, not for me!

ROBIN: He's our client.

NATALIE: Right, and I'm not your concern.

ROBIN: [*iPad*] Here's his contract. If you want homestyle I can do it again and bill for it under 'Extras'.

NATALIE: No I want him here to see me, overweight and nicotine-stained in the lobby of a suburban Westfield. I want the person I shared my life with for ten years to look me in the face and ask me to forgive him, and there's a good chance I won't. Clean and painless, no: it'd be ugly and shameful, it might even make things worse for a while. What I don't want is a robot spitting out fridge-magnet platitudes.

ROBIN: So … is that a yes?

NATALIE: What am I to him, a parking meter? Put in your spare change and walk away?

ROBIN: Oh I'm sure no, not a parking meter.

NATALIE: Does he feel absolved? Is that all it takes, reciting your Mastercard number over the phone?

ROBIN: He gave us a lot more than that.

NATALIE: Took out a line of credit, did he, for future stuff-ups?

ROBIN: No no, personal things.

NATALIE *scoffs*.

He told us about your life together, in some detail; how he felt about the situation,

NATALIE: Oh, he felt something?
ROBIN: Yes, and the things he once loved about you.
NATALIE: Did he now?
ROBIN: Yes, he did.
NATALIE: Like what?
ROBIN: He was quite specific.
NATALIE: So he spoke to you?
ROBIN: Not 'spoke', exactly. And not to me. There's an online form with a box at the end for extra comments—
NATALIE: A form.
ROBIN: … though I believe the mid-range has a 200-word limit.
NATALIE: Multiple choice.
ROBIN: Right, so like 'What problems has this action triggered?' Eg: 'addiction'. 'What kind of addiction?' You click on the appropriate one: 'alcohol; gambling; smoking'. 'What kind of smoking?': 'cigarettes; marijuana'—
NATALIE: Chewing-tobacco, his mouse must've slipped.
ROBIN: We compile all that information, process it through the template, and give it to the appropriate apologist to learn. Usually our recipients are very grateful.
NATALIE: Are they.
ROBIN: If you want to check out our website, you can read their testimonials.
NATALIE: And who writes those?
ROBIN: I— What? No, they're actual people.
NATALIE: So is my ex-husband. They'd be paying some company to write them.

    ROBIN *scrolls through pages on the iPad.*

ROBIN: Don't say that …
NATALIE: Feed the details into a template,
ROBIN: They're real, they're totally real, look at that, they can't even spell.
NATALIE: Homestyle.
ROBIN: No way, no way.
NATALIE: Look at them all, page after page of gutless wonders.
ROBIN: Give it back.
NATALIE: Have it, who cares, they're all yours, all—eight hundred and sixty four of them?

ROBIN: Most people lead busy lives.
NATALIE: Actually, do you know what, Robin? Thank God for you and your speech: I'm free of him. Go back and tell him to shove his multiple choice, 200-word, mid-range apology, and that he's given me a great idea for a novel.
ROBIN: [*off the iPad*] I would, except there's one problem. We've already guaranteed him a successful delivery.
NATALIE: So what?
ROBIN: If a client buys the warranty, we won't fail.
NATALIE: Hang on.
ROBIN: If he's paid for that, we don't need your signature.
NATALIE: You can't make me accept it.
ROBIN: No, we can't, but all we need in order to fulfil the contract is to have delivered the commodity in person, the implication being that you received it. I should've looked that up and saved us both a lot of trouble.
NATALIE: Won't he want to know how I took it?
ROBIN: [*scrolling through device*] Done, delivered, transacted—He ticked the 'no feedback' box.
NATALIE: But this was supposed to be a present, to me, he paid for the mid-range which isn't cheap, and what am I getting out of it?
ROBIN: The offer was made, you chose to decline.
NATALIE: But that's not fair, it's wrong,
ROBIN: I'm sorry ma'am.
NATALIE: You have to tell him I refused.
ROBIN: If you want to make a complaint you can take it up with your ex-husband.
NATALIE: No, I can't, I'm not speaking to him!
ROBIN: It's been a pleasure doing business with you. If you find yourself in need of our services, you have my card. We also offer a full range of very moving wedding toasts and eulogies. Meanwhile I hope you'll consider posting a testimonial on our website.

   ROBIN *makes to leave.*

NATALIE: No no no, this is bullshit!
ROBIN: Let go of me,
NATALIE: Take your stupid card and give me his contract—

ROBIN: Oh,
Please.
NATALIE: 'Give feedback', tick that box and tell him what I said.
ROBIN: Help! Somebody help me!

A scuffle over the iPad, in the process NATALIE *hits* ROBIN *in the face.*

Blood.

NATALIE: Oh …
ROBIN: Look.
NATALIE: Yes
ROBIN: I'm bleeding,
I can't see properly, everything's all blurry,
NATALIE: I—
ROBIN: My nose, oh my God oh my God, it's full of blood, it's pouring out.
What have you done?
NATALIE: Broken it, maybe
ROBIN: Help me, oh my God!

As ROBIN *turns in confused circles,* NATALIE *is torn. Then:*

NATALIE: I'll take your card. Okay?
ROBIN: There's blood on it,
NATALIE: I'll take this, and I'll call the company. That's what I'm going to do.
ROBIN: No, call an ambulance!
NATALIE: And I'll have them send someone along to represent me.
ROBIN: You can't just leave me, there's blood dripping on my iPad.
NATALIE: You'll get the bespoke. Don't you worry now.
ROBIN: I'm in agony.
NATALIE: I can see that.
ROBIN: You can't just walk away.
NATALIE: Clean and painless.

NATALIE detaches herself and leaves ROBIN *huddled on the ground, dripping blood on the iPad.*

END

DESERTCITYISLAND
Noëlle Janaczewska

Characters: TOUR GUIDE, ANTHROPOLOGIST, NEWCITY SPRUIKER

These three characters can be any age or gender. Feel free to cast in favour of women and diversity.

Punctuation and layout suggest rhythm and delivery.

The TOUR GUIDE *and the* NEWCITY SPRUIKER *speak 'DesertIsland Creole', a hybrid, international language. The* ANTHROPOLOGIST *speaks standard English.*

TOUR GUIDE: Sir, put backim chair! Please, suh.
Thank you, Sir.
Welcome to DesertIsland.
A cloudless cielo and—Look at that wow-wow beach!
Wunderbar, ja?
Tomorrow we will be driving,
in our petrol-saving Mitsubishi to the rainforest over-swarmed with description.
Tree after tree,
miles of eye snapping orchids.

Welcome Hapanese moon honeys.
Cherry tour bus and backed up Euro packers.
Welcome Merrycans with fat checked books.
Youse from Horsetrailer—I mean Horse-trailia—escaping your hum-a-day lives.
Carpe cervesa, oi-oi-oi!

Yes Sir, fizzy soda.
How do you like our shoe-shine sunset? Isn't she lovely?
Sorry about the wind, Sir, yessir, the wind is like the air only pushier.
ANTHROPOLOGIST: When the first ship docked here the language was different.

DESERTCITYISLAND: NOËLLE JANACZEWSKA

It began to change when the first aeroplane landed, and the local inhabitants hybridised a noun for money, so the boat people could talk to the plane people.

TOUR GUIDE: Bienvenue Mesdames, Ruski hookers,
big bananas here for the fishing lens porn,
très belles flat on their backs, while whitey GIs go press-ups on top.
While over there—Wowee! Native bambinos. Chucking yams
at the Merrycan planes
that zoong-zoong like a mosquito lost in your ear,
and keep your soul awake.
Si Senhor, of course terrorists might mix superglue with ladies' make-up, or preset iPhones with brainwashing messages.
Sir, don't you keep sitting on that chair passing glances. Please suh.
Thank you, Sir.

You enter the island with your ears, yes—?
through its music.
The clickety-chink of dishes
and silver
on the map-of-the-world buffet table.
See, that's where babushka went to clean toilets.
Duck! Mindim head, Madame.
Access rocky in music slum.
You enter the island through its music tours:
Original singing, tra, la, la—
Muchado praise the lording.
In nomine Patris, and all the rest of it.
A marchy band:
boom-boom, bang, crash, boom-boom.
Then eine kleine BBC news, and
Sayonara Senhor karaoke.

Look we have coming so many sightseeings upcoming to DesertIsland!
Hurry up females and sugar daddies, shop, shop.
There's the harbour of pirates centuries ago.
And here's Miss—thank you Miss Sing-along—

back from the store with a packet of curry-flavour.

Soon we'll be gassing the cooker, and mobiling the Mister in overseas.

No, I mean yessir. The biggest animals are in the sea because there's nowhere else to put them.

ANTHROPOLOGIST: One day the original inhabitants woke up and realised they'd shrunk. It didn't happen overnight, but it did happen—slowly. Because the border moves half a centimetre west every day, but so imperceptibly that—for reasons of whisky or whatever—the locals don't notice until suddenly a clothesline is over the limit, and they must re-tie the line.

As you've probably realised,

DesertIsland isn't actually an island in the true geographical sense.

TOUR GUIDE: Ciao bellissima!

Konnichiwa, members of the tourist race!

Come and join the party

diving into the gene pool

kids coming up coffee

papas' tears rolling down the cheeks

of their arses.

Fill up your deep throat at the island's

bottomless salad bar.

Absolut Monsieur, the king is customer here.

Sir, please.

Throwim back chair! Please suh!

Thank you, Sir again.

ANTHROPOLOGIST: On the eastern edge of DesertIsland lies the secular oasis of NewCity.

NEWCITY SPRUIKER: NewCity has become an alluring proposition for commerce and recreations. The desert city is the perfect gateway when if you are looking for modern sunshine and warmth on a par with other counterparts. The early months of the year also have the attraction added of the NewCity Shopping Festival. The smiling sea, the last resorts, the paramount of shopping experience and the taste of tradition all make NewCity the ultimate haven for delightful living citizens and travellers both. Shopping is not at all a new trend here. And you can enjoy your shopping extensively at conventional

bazaars or in NewCity's many air-conditioned complexes.
ANTHROPOLOGIST: Despite its architecture of enforced concrete and bullet-proof glass, NewCity is oddly without image. It cannot be imagined, yet thousands of Gastarbeiters—those nomads of the global economy—arrive every week to construct more retail plazas and office towers. And those migrants add their own verbal flavours to the language soup.
NEWCITY SPRUIKER: Turquoise waterways or camel tracks—your choice is irrespective. Remember that refuge can always be found in precincts and gated compounds. And respite may be afforded at random in settlements refashioned from past mayhem.
ANTHROPOLOGIST: Meanwhile, at the Airport huge cranes pick at the sky like giraffes.
NEWCITY SPRUIKER: When I first came to NewCity I was a frustrating experience. But no island is a man and now NewCity Airport has risen to great heights and is your gateway unfolding before you a huge treasury of the world's best sites and temptations. You want you can get flights from all the important countries to NewCity.
TOUR GUIDE: Irashimasu meinen Herren und Damen,
Ladies and gentlemen, public people,
We count your safety.
Mostly you will pass through villages
but at the Stadt border you can go a bit coconuts,
loco, kaput, let down your hair—Sir, please—
I said hair, not chair. Hair with an aitch, no see.
Now where was I?—ah, yes
Why not sushi up to some local colour?
Voulez-vous coucher, dah-dee-dah—
Blow up
condoms
with lipsticky kisses.
Comprende?
Yes Siree, the poor brown masses have a new face, and it's white. A washed out popping star.

Greetings and hail our tropical dis-Babel.
You want snap-snap—

you want pyramid of Luxor—
you want gay Paree—Voilà.
Tonight we are trying everyone delicious local fruit imported from
　Merrycan and Horsetrailer.
Don't you be worrying Missy
yesterday's atom test has been and done.
We're bulldogs beneath our tang-patterned sarongs
and still alive
with a future bright as the widening—
Heavens above!
It's Madame Doo-dah and Kojo.
Yes Sir, it's strange
that sometimes we cry when you're laughing.
ANTHROPOLOGIST: As well as being a foreign military base, DesertIsland has been home to several governments-in-exile. And these soldiers and political refugees contributed words for nostalgia and pickles to the language. And over time, that vocabulary has nudged out native expressions of happiness and fresh food. In DesertIsland so many words and colours have become trademarked that it's now almost impossible to speak without stumbling upon someone's trademark. Thereby breaking the newly instituted—and very strict—copyright laws.
TOUR GUIDE: Putee you in prison, lah.
ANTHROPOLOGIST: This restriction of the public lexicon has produced a kind of cargo cult on DesertIsland. Where the locals await a golden age when aircraft will fly in, loaded with the language of prosperity and new terms for independence.
TOUR GUIDE: In the litter of glory,
　after the vino and flag-waving
　and hours of hokey-pokey and conga muzak—
　enfin, finalamente
　adiós precious tourists and the alike,
　tschüβ, shalom, do svidániya, catch-youse-later.

We stood for while,
where our ancestors evaporated
without tombstones

in the peaceful grass,
wondering what comes next ...

END

EVELYN

Noëlle Janaczewska

Character: EVELYN, female, late teens or 20s.

Inner city Sydney circa 1935, and Evelyn is in trouble ... She's waiting in a police station—although we don't know that when the piece begins.

My preference is for any set to be minimal. Other than that, I leave it to the director and actor to make their own discoveries.

Punctuation and layout suggest rhythm and delivery.

EVELYN *knits as she waits—waits for what, we don't yet know.*

EVELYN: It could be worse.

    At least you know where you are with bad news.
    Good news nearly always carries a snag, a sting in the tale.
    Sooner or later you find out what it is, but til then, it lurks in the background
    ready to surprise you when you're least expecting.
    Whereas bad news means you know the worst straight away.

    It's the waiting that's hard.

    Should have known ...

    The frosted door-glass, the bolt thrown home.
    The muffled trade.
    But I liked the tilt of his accent, and when he kissed me it was easy to ignore the slithery pink in the whites of his eyes that spoke of too much drink. Easy to forget Kathleen Fowler's warning that he wasn't a stayer.

    Up on the height of the roof, near the stars—

'Got a surprise for you, Evie,' he said. 'Close your eyes. Go on shut tight. No peeking.'

Knit two together, purl four, to the end of the row.
The Devil makes work for idle hands. My Nan says that all the time.
Knit two, purl four …
When she reaches into the wool basket to unwind the yarn, I can almost hear the bleat of a newborn—

A just-born little lamb.
The bark of a sheepdog.
The breathing of a whole landscape of paddocks and dirt tracks and country women with sugar-dust on their hands.

The chanting of this skipping rhyme is heard in the distance. Faintly.

Needle to needle, and stitch to stitch,
Pull the poor woman out of the ditch;
If you're not out by the time I'm in,
I'll rap your knuckles with my knitting pin.

Back to Evelyn.
There's a strand of family gossip that says Nan's needles do more than knit.

Is it true? I ask Aunty Vi.
'Each sweater has its own story,' she says, holding up a front
of diamonds on a grey background.

Looks towards a closed door in the police station where she's waiting.

Any minute—

Waiting for the waiting to be over.

'Close your eyes, Evie,' he said.
And next I know there's this warm squirmy thing in my hand—

She giggles.

It's a rabbit!
He's given me a rabbit. It's brown and hungry and I call him George, and Mum and Aunty Vi will probably want him for the pot, but I won't let them.

'Now it's your turn, Evie,' he said. 'Your turn to give me something.'

I tease—
Tease out the knots and buried secrets of the wool basket. Send in questions like wolves to scatter the close-knit flock.
I'm trying to understand my Nan's life.
The design passed down the rows.

A hint of the skipping rhyme is heard in the distance. Still Faint.

Needle to needle, and stitch to stitch,
Pull the poor woman out of the ditch ...

I see things I'm not meant to.
Nan doing things with boiling water in the back room.
Hear things I'm not meant to.
About Bridie McCarthy who got septicaemia and died.
I see people who were never there.

'You know what I want, Evie,' he said. Runs his finger along my collar bone.
Giggles.
And the world goes toes up and topless.
An eel rises,
his tongue—
Giggles again.
His tongue tries its tip wherever ...

Afterwards I think: So much hurting to get to this moment.

Afterwards I can hear the end of someone's supper in a room below, spoons scraping bowls and talk gone ragged.
Listen to a storm starting up for the hell of it, hurling abuse at the walls.

We're not floating on a starry sea,
we're on the roof of a humdrum boozer.
The hot panting of souls and the stink of beer.

Afterwards I start counting—
purl one, knit two, purl—three days late ...
Kathleen Fowler says you can't make a man into a husband if it goes against his grain.
Goes to get up.
Then sits back down.
Glances again at the closed door in the police station.
Any minute—
but not yet. Not this minute.
Resumes knitting.
purl one, knit two, three weeks late ...

I knocked at the door with its frost-glass window.
The bolt thunders back.

'He's not here,' snapped a man with a face like a frog. 'He's a loose end, girlie. Shot though. End of story.'

The world explodes in a tempest of blood and indignation. Each stitch a gasp, a sharp point of pain.
Knit two, purl two, forty-four stitches down left side. The needle forced through the loop—Aah!
The chanting of the skipping rhyme. This time not so distant.

> *Needle to needle, and stitch to stitch,*
> *Pull the poor woman out of the ditch;*
> *If you're not out by the time I'm in,*
> *I'll rap your knuckles with my knitting pin.*

Aunty Vi drags me to church the following Sunday. To face off any rumours, she says.
There's Mrs Paxton knitting socks for Jesus. And the Minister telling everyone to seek God's forgiveness. I look at dust spinning in

the light coming through the stain-glass and wonder why God gives women such a rough time of it.

It's not fair.

We have to change George's name to Georgina. Part of me wants to get rid of her because she reminds me of him and that night on the roof and what happened three months later, but Mum says it's not fair to take it out on the rabbit.

Goes to stand up again.

Sits back down.

'Wait a minute, Missy,' the cop tells me. As if I haven't waited enough bloody minutes already.

Picks up her knitting.

Nan opens her door. She believes in her mission as much as the church Minister believes in his.
Wrong side facing, slip one, knit one, pass slipped stitch over.
She has her own homespun way of seeing things.
Her needle's plunge.
A harsh slip of a kiss, an excavation of red spoil and the woman feels a nameless spirit erupt from the pit of her being.
She knows the risks as she makes this particular stitch, the hot hook of a mother's choice.

I may have been on the receiving end of Nan's knitting, but it won't be me that unravels.
Like I say, with bad news you know where you are.
And I'm here to answer police questions.

'Remember,' Mum says, 'the art of the interrogator is to weave together not just what you say—the truth and the lies—but to assemble the silences.'

Check the tension,
and the directions taken by the eyes.
We recoil the yarn until we've got it straight and clear of tangles.

Because I've decided, afterwards, when we've done with the cops,
   I'm going to ask Nan—
to teach me her special knitting pattern.

Evelyn gets up.

Walks towards the door.

As she leaves, the skipping rhyme fades in. Now close by.

Needle to needle, and stitch to stitch,
Pull the poor woman out of the ditch;
If you're not out by the time I'm in,
I'll rap your knuckles with my knitting pin.

END

ROBINSON
Noëlle Janaczewska

Character: JACKIE, *female. Not too young, ideally nudging middle-age.*

Robinson *is about* JACKIE*'s relationship with a favourite book.*

The only prop needed is an iPad. Other than that I leave it to the director and actor to make their own discoveries.

Punctuation and layout suggest delivery.

JACKIE: When I need a bit of distance
   as you do sometimes,
   I escape to the ultimate desert-island fiction.

   My first *Robinson Crusoe* was a Penguin—or was it a Puffin? A birthday present from Aunty Gwen, who, like Crusoe, was an inveterate do-it-yourselfer.
   Shelves, socks, shortbread, Aunty Gwen made them all.

   Anyway,
   marooned on a tropical island, with nothing but common sense and a few salvaged tools, Robinson Crusoe organises nature. Builds a shelter, crafts furniture, bakes bread. The first lifestyle hero of DIY and good housekeeping—except there's no camera crew to film survival
   or otherwise.
   In fact for over half the book Crusoe's is the only voice—bar a parrot he trains to utter a few sentences.
   So until the larger world arrives, in the form of marauding cannibals, there's just the two of us: Robinson, and me the reader,
   and it's all very cosy.

   My university *Robinson* was a garage sale job lot—along with *Emma*, *Madame Bovary* and a couple of large-print crime titles.
   Crime, I've noticed, is often large print.

Unlike poetry which is always small.
According to our lecturer, *Robinson Crusoe* was the first work of modern realism written in English. But what sprouted in my head like a thistle was the recognition
that in twenty-eight years on his isle of despair,
twenty-five of them alone,
Crusoe is never bored.
Wow.

Sure, he speaks about chores and daily drudgery, but our contemporary craving for outside stimulation is absent.
In Literature One-O-One we learnt that novels developed as at-home entertainments for newly comfortable middle-class women with time on their hands.
In other words,
the English novel was born from the dust of boredom.

Imagine his island

green shoulders rising into cloud mass,

stink of goat.

Robinson number three was a borrowed hardback. I joined a reading group. We met every month at Fran's house. Some of us went because we were into books, and some because we were joiners—of anything.
Pilates, Indian cooking, Spanish for beginners.
What we were looking for wasn't so much insights into eighteenth-century fiction, we were there in Fran's kitchen looking for—I was going to say love, but no, that's wrong—

Community.

Yeah.

Community.

Maybe there amidst the chit-chat and Shiraz, was a new best friend?

Me, I was living with a boyfriend at that point. We broke up after I asked him what he thought about taking our relationship to the next level

and becoming friends.

People generally start there and become lovers, why not the other way around?

Eventually Friday comes.
And on page one-seventy of my Vintage Classic—*Robinson* number four—Crusoe teaches Friday to call him 'Master'— not usually a promising basis for friendship. But—and here's another brain thistle—the Englishman confesses more affection for his companion-cum-servant than he ever does for the family he left behind.
And Friday admits he would rather die than lose Crusoe.

By the way, I never got beyond the present in Spanish: I am, you are—
Shakes the hand of someone in the audience.
Hello, my name is Jackie.
And useless statements—unless I wash up somewhere with a lot of grey cats in trees, in which case I can announce: ¿Muchos gatos grises están en los árboles, sí?

No man is an island—I don't know who said that
but someone did.
I was
twelve years old,
hopeless at sports
awkward as a flagpole and devoid of friends, more or less.
Books became my bridge
to the mainland.

Along the way I became something of an expert in the genre
Tales of People Stranded on Remote Islands.

Christmas Island.

Nauru.

Manus Island.
*A few bars of The Andrews Sisters 1946 recording of the song
'Christmas Island'. Pianissimo.*

> *If you ever spend Christmas on Christmas Island*
> *You will never stray, for everyday*
> *Your Christmas dreams come true*
> *On Christmas Island your dreams come true.'*

What doesn't kill you makes you wonder ...

Back to *Robinson*.
Number four disappeared in another break-up
when we divided our books into His and Hers, *Robinson* went with
   him. I got *Bridget Jones*, *King Lear* and all the heavyweight
   Americans.

Crusoe survives his solitude because he cultivates his inner life and
   makes peace with his condition.

I survived adolescent loneliness
by mapping myself onto a whole heap of paper narratives.
Words filling up the empty horizon, waiting for life to come—to
   come to some kind of point.

Now people expect stories to happen to them. But I was changed by
   Mrs Dalloway and *Our Man in Havana*.

The problem with too much investment in the online world is there's
   no end of space, no end to searching for whatever floats your
   boat. So it's easy to find yourself a virtual Robinson Crusoe,
a castaway on a digital island.

But—in case you think I'm some kind of technophobe—*Robinson Crusoe* number five is an ebook.
See.

Shows the audience the ebook on her iPad.

There are films of course.

Flicks through the list on her iPad.

I've counted five adaptations. Including a sci-fi version set on Mars, and one directed by the Spanish surrealist Luis Buñuel.
You can catch some of the movies on this [*referring to the iPad*], but me,
I prefer to read.

The faintest hint of The Andrews Sisters 1946 recording of 'Christmas Island'.

You can watch a film, but you can live inside a book.
  ... On Christmas Island your dreams come true ... '

END

LONE BIRD

Verity Laughton

Characters:

STAN, *a boatman, any age*

ANANDA, *Sri Lankan, a passenger, mid 20s*

SUSAN, *Caucasian Australian, a passenger, mid 40s*

Set on a boat, on a river, in the dark.

A boat on a river leading towards a wall with some large gates. The river goes underneath a bridge at one point.

We don't actually have to see any of this.

It is night, the air is damp, but warm, the water oily and mysterious.

The boat seems small, but then again it might be large

STAN *is steering*

ANANDA: Where the fuck are we?
STAN: You usually talk like that to a stranger?
ANANDA: Sorry.
STAN: I've heard it all.
ANANDA: Then why'd you ask?
STAN: Sometimes I get tired of the sound of the water.
ANANDA: Water?
STAN: It takes a while.
    ANANDA *goes to the edge of the boat.*
ANANDA: I'm on a boat?!
STAN: What do you reckon?
ANANDA: Why am I on a boat?
STAN: You booked a ride? You stowed away? You've always wanted to travel by water?
ANANDA: I've been kidnapped.

STAN *laughs/snorts.*

STAN: Not by me you've not.
ANANDA: I am on a boat and I am on the water.
STAN: Einstein.
ANANDA: Fuck off.
STAN: I thought we talked about the language.
ANANDA: Fuck. Off.

The boat rocks.

ANANDA: I'm hallucinating.
STAN: You think?
ANANDA: I must be.
STAN: Is it likely?
ANANDA: Is it? Likely?
STAN: In a choice between a stuff up and a conspiracy always prefer the stuff up.
ANANDA: My name is Ananda … Ananda …

He can't think of the surname.

STAN: Yes?
ANANDA: Is my name Ananda?
STAN: If you say so.
ANANDA: Who are you?
STAN: Stan.
ANANDA: You're sure?
STAN: Stan-the-Man.
ANANDA: You're sure.
STAN: Sure I'm sure. I ought to know my own name, oughtn't I, Ananda? Is it? Ananda?

ANANDA *looks up at something way above them.*

ANANDA: What's that?
STAN: A bridge.
ANANDA: Hard to see in this light.
STAN: It's a bridge.
ANANDA: People! Crossing!
STAN: Yeah. Probably.
ANANDA: [*shouting up*] Hey!

ECHO: Hey! Hey! Hey!
STAN: They won't hear you.
ANANDA: Why not?
STAN: They never do.
ANANDA: Heeeeeey!
ECHO: Heeey! Heeeey! Heeeeeee …!

The boat rocks violently. ANANDA *sits very suddenly.*

ANANDA: I'm dizzy.
STAN: Yeah. Happens. Sit tight. Going past a bit of an eddy.
ANANDA: Eddy.
STAN: No, not 'Eddy,' sunshine, Ananda!

He laughs.

ANANDA: WHAT?!
STAN: Jesus. Look. It's an eddy, not a whirlpool see? Whirlpool's a different kettle of poisson, so to speak.
ANANDA: Poiss—
STAN: French, peasant.
ANANDA: Sri Lankans don't usually speak French!
STAN: Right.
ANANDA: Shut your face. I bet I speak more languages than you do. Peasant.
STAN: Yeah?
ANANDA: English. Tamil. Urdu.
STAN: Right.
ANANDA: Well?
STAN: Well what?
ANANDA: More than you, I bet.
STAN: Sorry to disappoint you but I've got a few more up my sleeve than that.
ANANDA: How many, then?
STAN: Don't you worry your pretty little head.
ANANDA: Listen mate—

SUSAN *sits up.*

SUSAN: My God.
ANANDA: Aaaagh!

SUSAN: Aaaagh!
STAN: You frightened him.
SUSAN: He frightened me.
STAN: Snap!
SUSAN: I thought I heard water through the bottom of the boat, it seemed so smooth and far away but then—
ANANDA: The eddy.
SUSAN: But then, bumpy—
ANANDA: That's it. The eddy.
SUSAN: A current pulling hard underneath—
STAN: She pulls all right. No motor, no oars!
ANANDA: [*realising for the first time*] No. No motor, no oars!
SUSAN: Water, not cold, oily almost, oily, slightly steamy water.
STAN: That's it. Water.
SUSAN: [*to* ANANDA] Do I know you?
ANANDA: No.
SUSAN: Are you sure?
ANANDA: Yes!
STAN: He's not really. Sure. Really, he doesn't know if he's Arthur or Martha. Or Ananda. He's already forgotten all his Urdu.
ANANDA: I have not!
STAN: No?
ANANDA: Ek, do, (*doe*) tin (*taan*) Ek. Do— uh— Ek … uh … uh
STAN: Yeah?

> ANANDA *mouths 'ek' but it feels strange to him.*

SUSAN: Don't worry. You're the only Indian here.
ANANDA: Sri Lankan.
SUSAN: I beg your pardon?
ANANDA: Sri. Lankan. You might remember it from such countries as Ceylon.
SUSAN: There's no need for—
ANANDA: Born in Colombo. Emigrated to Australia when I was three. We went to Mumbai when I was nine and I learned Urdu there. But then we came back here. I'm basically Australian. Basically.
SUSAN: It doesn't matter, you know. Neither of us mind that you don't.
ANANDA: Don't what?

STAN: Speak that language.
ANANDA: But I do!
SUSAN: I'm sorry but that wasn't Urdu. My husband speaks a bit of Urdu—he has business in India—he speaks just enough to get around—and I've been with him several times—and I've heard him—and that wasn't Urdu.
ANANDA: You're in on it.
SUSAN: On what?
ANANDA: The plot.
SUSAN: Plot!
STAN: Now what'd I say about stuff ups and conspiracies?
ANANDA: You and him.
SUSAN: I've never seen that man before in my life!
ANANDA: Then why are you on his *boat*!?
SUSAN: On his boat.
ANANDA: Yes.
SUSAN: Why am I on your boat?
STAN: You booked a ride? You stowed away? You always wanted to unravel by water?

ANANDA vomits over the side of the boat.

SUSAN: A bad sailor.

ANANDA vomits some more.

STAN: Dizzy.

ANANDA falls down motionless. He's vanished.

SUSAN: Where's he gone?
STAN: Wherever he's gone, I guess.
SUSAN: Is he still on the boat?
STAN: Possibly.
SUSAN: Why has he gone?
STAN: Lady, I just steer this boat.
SUSAN: Boat.
STAN: Yes.
SUSAN: Water.
STAN: Yep.

The sound of water.

SUSAN: Is it pretty by daylight? On this water?
STAN: Never seen it.
SUSAN: You imagine pools, and … overhanging trees, and dragonflies skimming the surface.

Pause.

Why am I on a *boat*?!
STAN: Calm down.
SUSAN: I want an explanation!
STAN: You booked a ride, you stowed away, you always knew one day you'd hobble to the water.
SUSAN: This is not a game!
STAN: It sure isn't.
SUSAN: Is this reality?
STAN: Whose?
SUSAN: Empirical reality.
STAN: Whose? Yours or his?
SUSAN: He's gone! [*Beat*] Or is it just a construction?
STAN: Yours or his?
SUSAN: I want an explanation!
STAN: That's all very well, but how do you want to *pay*?
SUSAN: [*beat*] I'm quite capable, you know. I'm used to managing on my own.
STAN: Oh, we're all lone birds on the water.
SUSAN: In the sky.
STAN: Sky?
SUSAN: Birds fly in the sky.
STAN: But the lone bird floats on the water.
SUSAN: [*beat*] You don't scare me.
STAN: That's what they usually say when the cold feeling hits them in the stomach. Or they faint.
SUSAN: Did I faint?
STAN: You fainted before. If the linguist's still here, then he may well have also fainted.
SUSAN: I fainted.
STAN: Yeah.
SUSAN: Why?
STAN: Fear?

SUSAN: Why am I afraid?
STAN: You might not have the wherewithal to pay.

Pause.

SUSAN: [*a bit panicky*] Joseph!
STAN: Here we go.
SUSAN: Where's Joe? [*Yelling*] Joe!
ECHO: Joe! Joe! Joe!

Silence.

The sound of water.

SUSAN: Where's my Joe? Where's my husband? Why am I here without my husband? What was I doing before I— Where's my Joe! Has he—fainted? Joe? Fainted?
STAN: No. I don't think so. Don't think I've got a 'Joe'.
SUSAN: [*calling*] Joe!
ECHO: Joe! Joe! Joe!

Silence.

SUSAN: Why am I afraid?
STAN: Gates up ahead.
SUSAN: Gates. [*Beat*] Where's Joe?
STAN: On a bridge somewhere?
SUSAN: No.
STAN: On the other shore?
SUSAN: The other shore. [*Beat*] Why is Joe on 'the other shore'?
STAN: Because we're all lone birds by the time we reach the water.

The sound of water.

SUSAN: What will happen at the gates?
STAN: The rest will wake. Those of you who can will pay me. Those who can't …
SUSAN: What happens to those who can't?

The sound of water.

SUSAN: I don't seem, [*looking*] to have any money [*looking*] on me [*looking*].
STAN: Then what will you pay me?
SUSAN: What happens if I don't?

STAN: What happens if you do?
SUSAN: I don't *know*!
STAN: No. You don't. Know. Do you?

The sound of water.

SUSAN: Where's that boy?
STAN: Mr Sri Lanka?
SUSAN: He'll do. Please? [*Beat*] Please?

STAN *kicks* ANANDA.

STAN: Wake up, you!
ANANDA: Where the fuck are we?!
STAN: You usually talk like that to a stranger?
ANANDA: Sorry.
STAN: I've heard it all.
ANANDA: Then why'd you ask?
STAN: Sometimes I get tired of the sound of water.
ANANDA: Water.

SUSAN *makes to speak.*

STAN *warns her off.*

STAN: [*to* SUSAN] It takes a while.

ANANDA *goes to the edge of the boat.*

ANANDA: I'm on a boat!
STAN: What do you reckon?
ANANDA: Why am I on a boat?
STAN: You booked a ride? You stowed away? You always wanted—
ANANDA: I've been kidnapped.

STAN *snorts.*

STAN: Not by me, you haven't.
ANANDA: I am on a boat and I am on the water.
STAN: Einstein.
ANANDA: Fuck off.
STAN: Thought we talked about the language.
ANANDA: Fuck. Off!

The sound of water.

I'm hallucinating.
STAN: You think?
ANANDA: I must be?
STAN: Is it likely?
ANANDA: My name is … my name is … What is my name?
STAN: [*beat*] Take her hand.

> ANANDA *takes* SUSAN *by the hand.*

[*To* SUSAN] Okay. Pay.
SUSAN: [*beat*] The warm fire in the living room.
STAN: Yep.
SUSAN: The babies in their cots long ago.
STAN: Yeah. Good.
SUSAN: The kookaburra on the wire this morning.
STAN: Nice touch.
SUSAN: Joe? [*Softly*] Joe …

> *She lets go* ANANDA'S *hand*

[*To* ANANDA] Thanks.

> *He slumps down, eyes closing. He's fainted.*

SUSAN: [*to* STAN] I am in the water.
STAN: [*quite gently*] Yeah.

> *The boat vanishes.*

> *She's floating.*

SUSAN: Floating in the water.
STAN: [*off stage*] Yeah.
SUSAN: [*fading*] In the water. Floating. [*Beat*] Water.

END

SIX O'CLOCK
Verity Laughton

Character: A YOUNG WOMAN, *post-World War I*

    It was dark when I got up and—
    the strangest thing—
    the light's on in the hall—
    must be all night while I was sleeping—
    must be Joe left it on and I must have
    drifted into sleeping—
    and I lean hard over
    the arm of the chair
    to turn the radio on
    — turn the radio on—
    — and I'm looking in the window
    — in the black glass window
    — and I see this woman's back
    — her sad, strong back
    — all white in the window—
    — and I think
    — what's that woman doing here?
    — in the dark?
    — before dawn?
    — in her tatty old clothes she must have slept in all night
    — what the— what's she *doing*?!

Then I realise it's me.

The light in the hall

hit the mirror in the cupboard
hit the glass in the window
hit me.

SIX O'CLOCK: VERITY LAUGHTON

I turn the radio on
then the lamp by the curtain
that Dan rigged up
and back into bed
with a copy of
just a copy of
True Confessions.
'I was the town's bad girl.'
Well. All right.
The picture of the woman
on the front
on the cover
it even looks like
a smarter version
a lot smarter version
of the woman in the bed
of me.

And the music stops and
the man on the radio says,

It's six o'clock.

And it hits me.

There's the flag on the wall
just above
the picture that we hung
when me and Dan
first found this place.
There's the flag on the wall
that Joe give me
at six o'clock when he
fucked me and he
kissed me and he
said goodbye.

And he said,
Boat's sailing at six o'clock,
will y' salute the flag

the stars and stripes
for the fucking and the kissing
that we've had this leave
will y' do that, Ella, will you do that for me?
Will ya?

And I think— Dan—
and
the light in the hall—
and
I think didn't
I think that
I saw a man
that made me think
of Dan down
by the harbour
by the harbour with Joe
Sunday evening?

And the radio chimes
six soft chimes
of six o'clock
and I salute Joe's flag
and I say to myself
to quiet my thinking,
Dan's dead in France and
I've his cap and his medal
to prove it.

And then it hits me.

Where are they?
Where've I put them?
I kept 'em in the cupboard
for the first six weeks
but they got in the way

so I put 'em on the mantelpiece
but that got too depressing
so I put 'em in the drawer of
Nanna Barton's dresser
but I kept bumping into 'em
and that was too depressing
too.

I must have moved them— oh— six times.

Under the bed.
I moved 'em under the bed.
Correction. True confession.
I kicked 'em there.

When?
Oh. The first Yankee sailor
that big blond boy,
the big one with the smile.
Yeah. Him.

Are they there now?
The cap with its silly little
medal like general distribution
medal like not something special
like just a silly little
medal tucked inside
the brim?

Well.
Can't think.
Mighta moved them.

Wassat?

Turn the radio off.

Just gone six o'clock.

Is that steps on the stairs?
Six of them?

I put it back on the chair—
True Confessions.
What's the point?
A confession?
He's dead and gone
old country boy Dan
and— true confession—
no-one's missed him.

I turn the light off.
Someone's on the landing.
Someone is on the landing.

I lie back in the bed.
I'm alone in the bed.

Then—steps on the stairs—
six more steps
up from the landing
six of them.
The flag on the wall
Six o'clock.

Why shouldn't I have a
flag on the wall?

The dark of the window
but— the light in the hall—
and there's a man at the door
and his mirror in the window
and I think— who is it?
Then it hits me.

END

SHOOTIN' THE BREEZE
Ned Manning

Characters:

DOT, *an old woman*

THEL, *an old woman*

The steps of a battered, weatherboard cottage in a working class suburb in the Great Depression. DOT *and* THEL *sit on a step.*

DOT: What's goin' on now?
THEL: Dunno.
DOT: Didya hear?
THEL: Oh yeah.
DOT: Funny.
THEL: Funny?
DOT: Like a kid's pop gun.
THEL: Didya see?
DOT: Nuh.
THEL: You?
DOT: Nuh. Doin' the washin'.
THEL: 'Course.
DOT: Smoke?
THEL: Ta.
DOT: Over there.
THEL: Where?
DOT: Across the tram track.
THEL: What's he doin?
DOT: Takin' a picture.
THEL: Look at me!
DOT: Give 'im a wave.
THEL: Nahh.
DOT: Go on.
THEL: Me hair.

DOT: Can't tell from there.
THEL: Might come over.
DOT: So?
THEL: Have ta tart up.
DOT: Why?
THEL: Never know.
DOT: No. Whatcha doin'?
THEL: You won't I will.
DOT: You're game.
THEL: Bloody snob.
DOT: Told ya.
THEL: Couldda waved back.
DOT: Too good for us.
THEL: Takin' pictures? Big deal.
DOT: They talk to you?
THEL: Yeah.
DOT: What you tell 'em?
THEL: Nothin.
DOT: Nosey bastards.
THEL: Yeah.
DOT: Look at 'em.
THEL: Think they own the place.
DOT: Flash car.
THEL: That's coppers for ya.
DOT: What's he doin' now?
THEL: Young fella?
DOT: What's he think he's doin'?
THEL: Takin' pictures.
DOT: Up there. Won't see nothin'.
THEL: 'Cept clouds.
DOT: 'N houses.
THEL: 'N us.
DOT: Go on.
THEL: What?
DOT: Give 'im another wave.
THEL: Got me pride.
DOT: Mighn't a seen ya.

THEL: I will if you do.
DOT: He might get ideas.
THEL: Wet behind the ears.
DOT: Give him a thrill.
THEL: Rude bastard.
DOT: He mighn't a seen us.
THEL: He's packing up.
DOT: Fair way away.
THEL: Look at 'im.
DOT: Might be scared.
THEL: Never even waved back.
DOT: Might think we're after something.
THEL: Bit of a wave wouldn't a killed him.
DOT: Coupla good sorts.
THEL: Us?
DOT: Yeah.
THEL: You got tickets.
DOT: I got washin' to bring in.
THEL: Yeah. Can't stand here gas-baggin' all day.

END

THE POLITICIAN
Ned Manning

Character: MAN, *a middle-aged politician on the top of his game.*
Set in his 'dressing room'.

A MAN *has just hopped out of the shower. He dries himself.*

MAN: Ahh that's better. That's what the doctor ordered. Might have gone a bit over time but who's counting? I haven't signed anything that's binding. I haven't signed any treaty! I gave 'in principle' support that's all. I said I supported it in theory. I covered all bases without committing myself. That's the trick you see. You don't want to go out on a limb and find yourself up shit creek without a paddle.

So, I pushed the envelope a little? I do it from time to time. In the privacy of my own home, of course. Never in public. You won't find me taking any risks in public. But here, away from prying eyes, I like to let my hair down a bit. Go a bit wild. Have longer than three minutes. Four. Five. Even six. As long it doesn't get out. As long as they can't pin anything on me.

Hey, come on, I gave myself a treat. No-one could say I didn't deserve it. You couldn't blame me, could you? After all the crap that's been thrown in my direction. At one stage there it was coming at me from all sides. It was raining shit and I was up to my neck in it. Not that I can't cop a bit of shit. I can cop whatever they throw at me. The more they throw the more I lap it up.

To tell you the truth, deep down I love it. It brings out the best in me. I've had sand kicked in my face since I can remember but I've always had the last laugh. You always do if you're a stayer. I just plough on until they lose interest or wear themselves out. Which they do. In the long run. It's a matter of who's got the most stamina. The most staying power. Most of them are fly by nighters. Here today gone tomorrow. I've seen plenty of them off. And I'll see plenty more off.

People wonder how I cope. It's easy if you've got the ticker.

If you're prepared to do the hard yards. This helps. A good old-fashioned shower helps. I get the gear off, turn the tap on. Make sure it's not too hot, not too cold. Wait till it's just warm enough and then I hop in and let it wash over me. I love watching all the crap disappear down the plug hole. Anti-clockwise.

If there's any really ingrained bits I get the Palmolive Gold and work up a good old lather and make sure I purge every orifice until I'm as clean as a whistle. Like this. A blank check. Ready to take on whatever is in front of me. I don't want any baggage, see? I don't want to be encumbered by yesterday's doings. I don't need the burden of built up expectation. I need to wash it away and start afresh. I need to be a clean slate.

I find it therapeutic too. The way the water massages you.

I'll let you in on a little secret. When I've had a big win, when I've really stuffed them, I often find myself getting a bit turned on in the shower. I think about how clever I've been, and I get a bit excited. I get up a bit of a lather and you know, give myself a bit of a work over. I don't do it all the time. Just when I've been especially clever. Like when I've deflected an assault from some arsehole in the media. Or when I've come up with a way to euchre my enemies.

He puts on his underpants. They have an Australian flag on them.

You see I'm not hampered by ideology. I'm not beholden to anyone. Except myself. That's why I love a bit of a tug. It's reminds me who I'm in this for. For myself. I mean, if you can't please yourself, who can you please?

That's where the others stuff up. They're always trying to please other people. They don't get it. If you're only in it for yourself, you can do anything. You can say anything. Your hands aren't tied. They're free to roam.

This water business is a case in point. As if it's going to run out while my arsehole's pointing to the ground! There's plenty of water. For the time being. They come at me from all sides about it but I just bat them off. I smile and nod and think about the shower I'm going to have. That's the trick, see? Getting the balance right.

I'll give you an example. I was down in bloody Tasmania the other day. Breaking bread with the inbreds. God knows why we colonized the joint in the first place. It's nothing but trouble. Anyway, they had me walking around some forest and I had to pretend to be interested in the bloody trees. Mosquitos buzzing round like journalists on heat, it was hell. I had the Akubra on, of course. The girls reckon I makes me look like an outdoorsy type. Reckons the inbreds like it. Makes me look like I'm one of them. That'll be the bloody day, but I'll tell you something for nothing, I'll wear anything for a vote.

So, I'm standing there, looking up at this bloody great tree and they're banging on about the environment and old growth forests and shit and I'm thinking,

'There'd be a few dollars in that thing. If you cut it down.'

I'm always thinking, see? I'm thinking while I'm nodding at the smelly bearded bloke who's banging on about greenhouse and carbon dating and God knows what else. I'm thinking pulp, woodchips, floorboards, whatever. I'm thinking about the shower I'm going to have while I'm smiling at this evolutionary throwback. I shake his limp wristed hand and wave goodbye to the greenies.

Ten minutes later I'm having my fingers crushed by another smelly bearded bloke but this one's a timber cutter. He's as rough as guts and scares the shit out of me. I imagine him with a chain saw gleefully going through what's left of the population of Port Arthur. I laugh at his moronic jokes and assure him and his Neanderthal mates that the timber industry's safe on my watch. It occurs to me that talking to them is about as interesting as talking to a bit of wood. I promise them that I won't let them down and that understand their concerns and then I'm out of there.

All in a day's work, see?

He puts on a crisply ironed shirt.

Today's different though. Today's the big one. Today's the day that turns it all around. The day the big guy rides into town. And I'm going to be ready to greet him and shake his hand and look him in the eye and say,

'Welcome dude.'

And he's gonna smile and pat me on the back and everyone's gonna be so proud of me. The cameras will go off and all round the world they'll see me holding hands with the leader of the free world.

Me. In my own back yard. I'll tell you something for nothing, I won't be dragging him round any bloody forests that's for sure. I'll be looking after the dude. Putting my best foot forward.
    And I'll be looking my best too. It's why I'm wearing this.
    He puts on his tie. More Australian colours.
I was given this. By the Wallabies. The footballers. They gave it to me. Pretty good eh? A Wallaby tie. Not everyone gets to wear one of these. He'll be impressed. He'll think I'm sporty. He likes sporty types. He's like me. Hates all those arty farty types. Nothing but trouble. Not like footballers. They talk our language.
    Looking good eh?
    He puts on his suit trousers.
I've turned the place upside down, so he feels right at home. Made sure everything's in order and up to scratch. Cleared the decks and erected the barricades.
    Pity we don't go in for that type of thing. Motorcades and big parades and choppers hovering and fear in the air. I like it. Makes me feel, I dunno, big. Like being in a movie. A war movie. A proper one. Not one of those harping bits of left-wing propaganda that titillate the chattering classes. No way. A real man's movie. A John Wayne one. One when you know who's a goody and who's a baddy. One where the good guys win and the bad guys it in the neck. Just as it's meant to be. He loves John Wayne movies. So do I. We watch them at his ranch while the girls swap recipes. It's so good. A couple of cans of coke, some good ol' popcorn and we're like a couple of pigs in shit.
    Puts on his shoes and socks.
I love giving the police something to do too. Give 'em a sense of purpose. A chance to sharpen their skills and test their mettle. It's fantastic. They're everywhere. They're on a mission and they've got me to thank for it. With any luck they'll be a bit of trouble and they can discharge their duties and win me an election.
    I like a shiny shoe, don't you? Says something about a guy. Says he's got authority. And class. And knows which side his bread's buttered on.

He puts on his coat and smooths down his hair.

You're looking at a winner. A guy who knows what to do when the chips are down. A guy who knows exactly which side his bread's buttered on. A guy who can sniff out a victory when there's none in sight.

Checks his watch.

So here we go.
What lies can we tell today?

END

THE FAMILY NAME
Catherine Zimdahl

Characters:

An elderly FATHER, *two young adult* CHILDREN, *female or male*

Gothic sensibility.

The FATHER *stands, his body contorting in tormented shapes, his face freezing with soundless screams.*

The CHILDREN *enter and stare at him.*

CHILD 1: Father?
CHILD 2: Dada.

> *The* FATHER *becomes conscious of them. He reaches out his hands to them.*

FATHER: My blessed progeny.

> *He touches their faces.*

CHILD 1: Father? What ails you?
FATHER: Thoughts. Thoughts. Thoughts and an action.
CHILD 2: Ah Dada—a new idea, yes? Yes? Yes? Another trap? Give people what they want and starve them of what they need.
FATHER: Beyond.
CHILD 2: Sounds brilliant!
FATHER: Have you ever seen our existence in crystallized form?
CHILD 1: Momentary experiences mostly in nature.
CHILD 2: [*laughing*] The tyranny of irony!
FATHER: No, the tyranny of tyranny.
CHILD 1: Father, you'd tell us if something was wrong.

> FATHER *turns to* CHILD 1.

FATHER: Your hands are so soft. [*Pause.*] The rivers of gold will no longer course around us rather we will be a beacon of love.
CHILD 2: That is is all a bit obscure and mystical even—

CHILD 1: He could have a fever. He's altered. I can call Doctor—
FATHER: A doctor cannot heal this sickness.
> *He looks at them both.*

When you were young I gave you the history of the world.
CHILD 1: Yes. How we won, Father, yes, I well remember it.
CHILD 2: We are the Holy Roman Emperors, the King of Kings of Majesties—
CHILD 1: Pharaohs and Dynasties—
CHILD 2: Presidencies of Democracies and Dictatorships.
FATHER: Yes.
CHILD 2: We built the Pyramids, the Colosseum, the White House, the Great Wall of China and countless clueless colonial countries that didn't stand a chance.
FATHER: In blood to break the spirit, in blood to—
CHILD 2: It takes decisive leadership, Dada, to see an individual as so totally devoid of humanity to—
CHILD 1: [*to* CHILD 2] Shush!

> FATHER *takes his hands from his* CHILDREN *and covers his face exhorting to God in Latin in prayer (see end note).*

Father you may feel that all your hard work is for naught but let me assure you that we are the wealth creators. We have enabled and ennobled the vast majority of families to build their lives and futures. I can bring up the numerals if you wish.

> *The* FATHER *says the 'prayer' again faster and more distraught.*

CHILD 2: He's babbling.
CHILD 1: It's some kind of Latin prayer—
CHILD 2: He's possessed.
CHILD 1: For God's sake. No.
CHILD 2: Dada. Let's go elephant hunting. You always feel happy when you kill—
FATHER: I have never been a happy man!
CHILD 2: You always say it, say it Dada, say it—'We have the world in our thrall.' Except for the odd firebombing people applaud, they think they are thankful! 'We have the world in our thrall.'
CHILD 1: We research and develop new medicines, helpful inventions and—

CHILD 2: [*whispering into* FATHER's *ear*) Secretly everyone wants a slave.
FATHER: There is a cold current of electricity zapping the life out of every single thing we touch! This is why it ends here.

The CHILDREN *look at each other.*

CHILD 2: Dada I am very sorry for losing the private island in Fiji in that poker game—
CHILD 1: I don't think he is referring to that.
FATHER: The research has been completed. The names of the lost have been found. The families will be advised all 43,000 descendants from our forebear's property of 9862 slaves. With a stroke of a pen all our financial interests will be consolidated from havens to bolt-holes from mines to mattresses and—

Pause.

Is it not a thing of beauty!?
CHILD 1: Yes ... yes.
FATHER: Doesn't it want to make you weep with the justice of it all?!
CHILD 1: Yes.
CHILD 2: I'm calling Doctor—
CHILD 1: Shh. No. It makes perfect sense Father. He's perfectly sane.
FATHER: And furthermore our Family Trademarked Name will be replaced and we will be known forevermore as 'Thatviciousrapingmurderingslaveowningfamily'.
CHILD 2: That's our name! That's who we are— that's— that's our birthright, that's what— what— we live up to!
FATHER: Precisely. That's our Brand. It's only apt.
CHILD 1: I have spent a lot of time considering these issues and I feel as upset as you do Father but I do believe we can make a difference. However instead of focusing on the past why not the present and the future? So I would suggest that we have a private foundation to address the scourge of modern-day slavery. I think we could have a positive impact.
FATHER: Rid of it all! Every cent!
CHILD 1: No, no, no, Dada Dada Dada no! Where would I go?
FATHER: Both of you have had the best education, opportunities and connections surely—

CHILD 2: We will be expunged from the guest list of our circles. Our peers will never forgive us for this— this— this precedent—
FATHER: It will break the curse.
CHILD 2: Oh please! That bullshit curse. It's just one of those shabby Vanity Fair articles— tabloid pap for poor people to say how lucky they are. We have exactly the same suffering in our family as any other. We just die in extravagant and exotic ways.
CHILD 1: Calm down.

   Pause.

FATHER: Do you hear that?
CHILD 1: It's the wind that's all.
FATHER: It is swirling around inside me.
CHILD 2: Let's call an ambulance.
CHILD 1: No.
FATHER: Where is my pen? The pen passed down and still with the bloody fingerprints on it.

   He slowly takes the pen out of his breast pocket and gazes at it.

CHILD 1: Dearest Father, I am concerned as you are in restoring public trust in our organisation and its relationship to the past. The ideas that you are referring to are no longer acceptable in any form. We must commission a report before all stakeholders have sadly passed away. This can, as we know, unfortunately take time to be exact and farsighted. But in the meantime there must be a ceremony and apology and it must be heartfelt or it means nothing. The problem is— the difficulty and it must be discussed is that underprivileged people do not know how to handle money. What they need is education. We could distribute funds to our University for scholarships—
CHILD 2: Drugs. Hangers on. Pimps. Sex. Indulgence. Bad judgements. Suicides. Death by misadventure. It's all we were warned about and now you want to present it as a gift. You may as well be giving them the pox.
FATHER: It's not a gift. It is reparation. And I have pondered, meditated and asked the great stars for guidance. I've communed with the dead I have, can you hear them? My nights and days wrecked by dark visions of all that was done in our blood. And you my blessed progeny will be absolved, set free with a stroke of my pen.

Pause.

Furthermore—

CHILD 2: Oh, there's more?

FATHER: You will be compelled to visit each descendant's family on the anniversary of my passing and you will sit with said descendants and listen to the stories of their lives and if they command you to serve them you will because that is now the way of your life and you will wash their feet if they so ask and this will be the way of your life forever more.

CHILD 1: But if it is not done with love but rather fear?

FATHER: Then that is the truth.

CHILD 1: And if they deprive us of our liberty.

FATHER: Then that is the truth.

CHILD 1: And if they wound and kill us?

FATHER: Then that is the truth.

CHILD 2: What happened to the cold calculating man cutting his way through life? Creating traps for our enemies? The man I aspired to be?

FATHER: I'm absolving you.

CHILD 2: No, you're a walking deathbed conversion. Turning us into slaves conflating our fate with theirs.

FATHER looks out beyond them into the audience area.

FATHER: They are coming for us.

CHILD 2: [*sobbing to the* FATHER] I am useless. I know nothing. I can't do—

FATHER: They are there staring. Look can you see them? They are coming!

CHILD 1 takes off their belt and whips the ground.

CHILD 1: Yah! Yah! Yah!

CHILD 2: [*sobbing harder*] Dada don't you love us? Please please love us.

CHILD 2. runs to his FATHER taking his hand and kisses it.

CHILD 1: Yah! Yah! Yah!

CHILD 1 then comes up behind the FATHER and grabs the pen from the him. He shoves it against the Father's neck artery. At the same moment The FATHER throws CHILD 2 to the ground and stamps his boot on his neck hard. Turns to face CHILD 1. *The* FATHER *laughs a great guffaw.* CHILD 1 *slowly takes the pen away from his neck.*

FATHER: Ah my darling child you are the one. You have won. I can die assured that our glorious family name will viciously live on.

They stare out to the audience.

FATHER/CHILD 1: Yah! Yah! Yah!

END

End note: The FATHER*'s prayer behaves like a Latin exorcist prayer but it isn't. It is a boast of delight in his own depravity and evil. It is up to each production to create this prayer. It must be another trick by the* FATHER *to convince his* CHILDREN *he has gone mad.*

HERENOWTHENTHERE
Catherine Zimdahl

Characters:

RODRIGO, *late forties to fifty*

SHADOW, *male, a protean force*

CAT, *puppet operated by* SHADOW

RODRIGO*'s interior experience is conveyed through music, lighting and projection.*

Sound design ranges from Chilean folk, to electric, distortion, feedback and minimalism.

RODRIGO *stands casting a* SHADOW, *in the shadow lays another man—his* SHADOW.

RODRIGO: There's a white light inside of me.
No-one can see it but I feel it.
No-one can touch it.
Nothing can get to it. It's mine.

> RODRIGO *walks forward but as he does so the* SHADOW *grabs his foot, he falls flat on his face.*
>
> *The* SHADOW *drags him up, parallel to him but* RODRIGO *is upside down.*
>
> *Slowly they form a ball and roll together ending up both in a standing position.*

SHADOW/ADVOCATE: Please take a seat.

> *The* SHADOW/ADVOCATE *guides* RODRIGO *to a chair.*
>
> RODRIGO *looks around, startled, then sits down.*

SHADOW/ADVOCATE: In your own words. [*Kindly*] Look them in the eye otherwise they will think you are lying. This is your opportunity to make your case to the Tribunal.

> RODRIGO *cannot bring his gaze up. He looks petrified.*

They won't think you are genuine. That you can't return.

> RODRIGO *raises his eyes, breathless.*
>
> *The sound of a typewriter. The lilt of an acoustic guitar rises up.*

RODRIGO: There, there was an official to interrogate.
There was an agent to torture.
And someone with a typewriter to record it.
There was a guard playing guitar outside.
There's a shuffle of papers.
The closing of a door.

> *The distinctive sound of this door closing.*
>
> *At this sound* RODRIGO *pushes back his chair and reels back, staggers onto the ground, arms splayed. The* SHADOW *mirrors him, hovers over him, arms outstretched, sinister.*

But I am loved.
I don't know by what.
I look at Christ on the cross.

> *The* SHADOW's *arms slowly outstretch to become Jesus crucified.*

Christ tortured on the cross.
I think it's good that he died.
Didn't have to live on.

> RODRIGO *reaches up and gently takes Christ/*SHADOW *down from the cross. Cradles him. The* SHADOW *turns into a* GIRLFRIEND, *sits up slowly, reaches in close to him.*

She said the first time—

SHADOW/GIRLFRIEND: Your country is definitely on my list of countries to do before I die. I love the music, the culture, the men.

> *She stares at him.*

RODRIGO: She said the first time we were alone—

SHADOW/GIRLFRIEND: Tell me a secret you've never told anyone.

> *The* SHADOW/GIRLFRIEND *reaches over and strokes his neck.*

RODRIGO: [*alarmed*] What, what are you capable of?

> *He takes the* SHADOW/GIRLFRIEND's *hand from his neck.*

SHADOW/GIRLFRIEND: I think maybe I'm capable of loving—
RODRIGO: The violence in your eyes.
SHADOW/GIRLFRIEND: [*flummoxed*] Pardon?
RODRIGO: What are you capable of??

The SHADOW *grabs* RODRIGO *by the neck and drags him back to the chair.*

SHADOW: What am I capable of? Capable. 'Capable' this word implies a minimal proficiency. I have excellence. The precise pain, in the precise place, the precise amount for the desired effect to leave you living in a land somewhere between life and death.

The sound of the door closing.

RODRIGO: Murder my memories, murder my memories, murder my memories.

Pause.

Some days I go for days without talking and my thoughts feel outside my head filling a room. And everyone can see into me. And the sounds of the world cuts into me. There's a darkened room, to wait it out until the senses come back to you. And you search for that white light. Because if there is a God, God will give it to you. And when all is gone and you are empty as sin you feel this will, this will of God and you have information, a message from Jesus and you weep with all the suffering he felt. How he absorbed the suffering of the world. And you walk the streets and there's a man with restless hands and the buzz off him knocks the breath—

He flinches.

And then you're in hospital and they're telling you you're nothing, God didn't touch you—he left you alone and there is no beginning or end to electricity, a burst of colours spitting out of me. And you'll tell them anything or the one thing that led your comrade to his death and you have to live with it knowing you lived. And you got to a new country to start again. But wherever you are there is no now or there or here or then.

The SHADOW/THERAPIST *sits facing him.*

I can't, I can't breathe—

In the following, dialogue comes in and out of volume, like a phone call breaking up. Words in italics are louder.

SHADOW/THERAPIST: Your *breath is too high* in your chest, breathe *deep, down* into your diaphragm. *Use your senses*, feel *the ground* beneath your feet. Your hands, *unfurl your fists*, breathe deep, hear the birds in the trees, bring yourself *into the room*, the ticking of the clock like *a heartbeat*, bring your eyes to mine, *breathe* deep into *the present*. No need to fear here, in this moment, you can *tell me anything*.

RODRIGO: Broken?

SHADOW/THERAPIST: No. I know you *have the strength*.

RODRIGO: I can't, I can't hear, the words— what have you said?

SHADOW/THERAPIST: It takes *time* and *talk* and *rest*.

RODRIGO: My head, my head …

> *Long, long, pause. The* SHADOW *transforms, comes round the back of him.*

But I am loved.
I don't know by what.
I have a job; it's not much of a job for someone with very good English. Excellent English isn't enough when I look too tremulous to trust.

> *Pause.* RODRIGO *begins to clean as he speaks, very methodically, in stylized movement. The* SHADOW *tails him, a chaotic figure, gradually undermining him, pushing his hands away from his tasks …*

I clean. I work for upper-middle class families with pure-bred dogs, Aboriginal art and ethnic cleaners.
They leave the money on the table.
They never see me.
A life beyond me.
The toys, the newspapers, the family photographs to be dusted. Are they as happy as they seem? I vacuum up the bits of biscuits the baby has left.
Their busy days.
The fridge full of reminders to return the books to the library,

swimming lessons, fingerpaintings, children's parties …
Civilisation, a house, children, a heritage.
I find it comforting that this world exists.

    RODRIGO *looks lost.*

I was once a Marxist, have I become this?

    He looks up at the SHADOW. *The* SHADOW *begins to push him.*

I, I have beliefs.
SHADOW: You had beliefs.
RODRIGO: I have beliefs.
SHADOW: But now you can't think them through. You can try to turn personal pain into political dignity but we won. We've colonized you. You're a country without a flag, a mascot, an anthem.
RODRIGO: [*struggling with the* SHADOW] A nation … is … judged … by … the … way … it … treats … its … people!

    RODRIGO *pushes the* SHADOW *then tackles him in a headlock furiously to the ground, sucking the life out of him until* RODRIGO *reels back, fearful of his anger, fearful of what he is capable of.*

    RODRIGO *walks around and around, trying to calm himself down.*

I have days and days, great days.
    I walk at dawn, just walk and walk and, and, and I realize for that moment I have no fear. And all the dew on the leaves glisten—white light, what's the word— 'refracted' and reflected.

    He pushes the SHADOW *harder.*

And I flow with water, awoke in water, and I know—we are water, streams, rivers, all oceanic.

    The SHADOW *is pushed even harder, falls to the ground.*

And I know that's where we go, when we pass and die, we leave behind this scrap of dirt we weep and suffer for and we live, we live in everything.

    The SHADOW *laughs at him.* RODRIGO *stands alone, lonely.*

    RODRIGO *walks over and sits down next to the* SHADOW.

She said, she said—

    SHADOW *as* GIRLFRIEND *takes his hand gently.*

SHADOW/GIRLFRIEND: [*softly*] Tell me a secret you've never told anyone.

He looks away, she follows his gaze, he looks back at her, then away, but she is tracking his eyes.

RODRIGO: And her eyes were wide open holding me like a home.

He looks into her eyes for a long time.

I say the cliché— 'the, the, the coups are the worst, the first forty-eight hours ... [*Gathering himself*] In the middle of the night ...' I hear myself saying so easily 'subjected', 'suspended' 'the shocks' 'the shame' 'the shit and piss'. 'Children, children singing in the playground across the way, can they not hear the screams?' But I want to be known. I talk, talk, talk spilling out of me, feeling good, better, great, lighter ...' The guard that came with paper and pen 'You must write your last wishes', condemned, he screws up the paper, hood over my head and shuffled in circles and back again, dazed, cold, steel [*mimicking a gun*] on my neck. Get ready for this. Ask God for grace the guard says and I wait for the crack! [*Pause*] A click. That's it. No. The *thumping* in my chest. I'm not *dead*. I'm not *dead*!'

RODRIGO *looks up at her. Long pause. She looks ashen.*

'Don't go please don't go.' Afraid. I tell her I was astonished, bewildered at the cruelty— 'I, I would never hurt any living being.' And with the way she takes her bag and holds it to her body she says—

SHADOW/GIRLFRIEND: Now I can't not know.

The SHADOW/GIRLFRIEND *gets up slowly, goes.*

The sound of the closing door.

RODRIGO: [*fast*]There's a white light inside of me.
No-one can see it but I feel it.
No-one can touch it.
Nothing can get to it. It's mine.

Pause. SHADOW *manipulates* CAT, *around his legs,* RODRIGO *lies down, totally relaxed.*

She was a stray, she came to my window one day. Happy to be in my home. I bought the best cat food I could afford. Playthings, toys! At night she would disappear out the window but always, always be on my chest in the morning looking into my eyes as I awoke, purring, welcoming me to the world, my cat.

He rests, sleeps then startles.

I don't remember when, but I woke and she wasn't on my chest. She was shivering at the end of my bed. I called and she didn't come. Her eyes glazed and alone. I didn't know what was wrong. I raced her to the vet.

The SHADOW *becomes the* VET *handling the* CAT *carefully.*

She didn't know what was wrong. A fever maybe. Please don't take her away.

The Vet turned her over. We gasped. On her sweet pink and white [*gesturing to his stomach*] was a boot-shaped blue and purple bruise.

SHADOW/VET and RODRIGO: Why would someone kick such a beautiful being?

Long pause.

RODRIGO: We didn't know whether she would live.
There were tests.
The kidneys.

The SHADOW/VET *takes the* CAT *away.*

They said go home. I waited. Antiseptic room.
Her ribs were broken. I waited.
I could take her home.

RODRIGO *rolls over on the ground, flat completely relaxed. His cat on his chest. He pats her, she purrs.*

Pause.

There is a clap of thunder and flashes of lightning. He startles, feels his chest, she's not there. He gets up and searches.

I called, I called for her, feared and found her cowering on the cold, bathroom tiles where they washed the blood away. I say over and over again 'I will never give you up'. The thump of the sky. Shiver.

I stayed with her stroking her— 'I know, I know it's not fair they have brought you here.'

The SHADOW/CAT *slowly, carefully pads up* RODRIGO'S *arm to look deeply into his eyes.*

Pause.

And when the storms come, I cannot fight the sky for you. No puedo luchar contra el cielo port i. I can only be alive for you.

END

APPENDICES

PRODUCTION NOTES

DONNA ABELA
Aurora's Lament

Aurora's Lament was commissioned by the ABC for the *Old Texts Revisted* series, produced and broadcast on Airplay, Radio National in 2009, and won the 2010 AWGIE Award for Radio Adaptation.

Stella Started It

Stella Started It was part of 7-ON's *Platonic* project which was presented at NIDA in 2012, and the 2019 Storytellers' Festival at Kings Cross Theatre.

VANESSA BATES
That Night We Lost Jenny

The Night We Lost Jenny was broadcast as a radio play by Eastside Radio as part of their Sonic Tales program in 2012.

Small Hard Truths

Small Hard Truths was originally produced by Bondi Feast 2012 and in 2021 for Newcastle's Micro Theatre.

HILARY BELL
Cheering Up Mother

Cheering Up Mother was written for a group project at Juilliard in 1997. Its Australian premiere was in 2005's Short + Sweet Festival (Sydney).

The National Apology Centre

The National Apology Centre was written for 7-ON's *Seven Social Sins* project. It is a response to the social sin 'Commerce without Morality'.

NOËLLE JANACZEWSKA
DesertCityIsland
DesertCityIsland was written as part of 7-ON's *This Island's Mine*.

Evelyn
Evelyn came out of 7-ON's *Long Shadows* workshop at the Sydney Theatre Company. It was produced by Short + Sweet (Sydney) in 2018.

Robinson
Robinson was written as part of 7-ON's *Platonic* project which was presented at NIDA in 2012.

VERITY LAUGHTON
Lone Bird
Lone Bird was written for Brand Spanking New, a New Theatre (Sydney) initiative in 2009.

Six O'Clock
Six O'Clock was written for 7-ON's *Long Shadows* workshop at the Sydney Theatre Company.

NED MANNING
Shootin' The Breeze
Shootin' the Breeze was written for 7-ON's *Long Shadows* workshop at the Sydney Theatre Company.

The Politician
The Politician was written for 7-ON's *Seven Social Sins* project in response to the sin 'Politics without Principle' and performed as part of Brand Spanking New at the New Theatre in 2009.

CATHERINE ZIMDAHL
The Family Name
The Family Name was written as part of 7-ON's *Seven Social Sins* project. It was a response to the social sin 'Wealth Without Work'.

APPENDICES

The Family Name was first produced by Subtlenuance Theatre Company in 2021 as part of the *Morning Star* multi-playwright project.

HereNowThenThere

HereNowThenThere was created as part of 7-ON's *This Island's Mine*. It was first produced at the Brand Spanking New Festival in 2009.

7-ON PROJECTS

7-ON is a group of playwrights who came together in 2005. We create work as a group and also support each other's individual projects. We see ourselves as seven minds that don't think alike but are simpatico in this—our belief in the transformative properties of our artform and its place in Australian culture.

Most of the scripts in *Sharp Darts: Chamber Plays by 7-ON* have been taken from 7-ON collaborative projects.

7-ON's first project was *The Seven Needs*—seven short plays based on Abraham Maslow's hierarchy of needs. They were produced at Griffin Theatre in 2006 when then Artistic Director Nick Marchand paired them as short opening plays with main season offerings. The plays were later published by Currency in *Short Circuit*, an anthology of Griffin-premiered scripts.

In 2008 came *Old Texts Revisited*— a series of radio drama pieces commissioned for the ABC with a view to the Prix Marulić International Festival of Radio Plays and Documentary Drama.

7-ON co-wrote a script outline inspired by Nietzsche's *Thus Spake Zarathustra,* as a basis open to further devising for the drama students at the University of Wollongong. Called *All or Nothing* this 'adaptation' had a workshop production at the University of Wollongong in 2008 directed by Chris Ryan.

In 2009, 7-ON wrote a series of pieces under the title of *This Island's Mine* with State of Play. In the same year we researched and wrote a large work as part of a residency with the Sydney Theatre Company, inspired by Historic Houses and Peter Doyle's photographic exhibition 'City Of Shadows' at Sydney's Justice and Police Museum. This evolved into *Long Shadows,* a development directed by Lee Lewis.

In 2011, 7-ON contributed short works, mostly monologues, for an independent showing entitled *I Contain Multitudes*, directed by Augusta Supple at Theatre 505 in Sydney. In the same year, 7-ON was instrumental in advocating for the Solutions Roundtable for female playwrights held by the Australia Council, as well as holding a Playwrights' Muster at Griffin Theatre.

In 2012, 7-ON published a book of monologues for drama students, *No Nudity, Weapons or Naked Flames*, through Federation Press. Like much of our individual work, this publication is also available from Australian Plays Transform (apt.org.au). A number of the monologues in the book were part of a production at the Tap Theatre by Augusta Supple and Jeremy Waters in 2013. The show was called *Mayday Playwrights Festival: No Nudity, Weapons or Naked Flames*.

In 2013, following a 2012 reading at NIDA, 7-ON continued to work on *Platonic,* this time during a residency at Hothouse Theatre's farmhouse in Albury. *Platonic* was our response to the question: What is friendship in the twenty-first century?

In 2015 came *We are the Ghosts of the Future*, a one-hour immersive theatrical experience that unfolded across a Victorian warehouse at The Rocks, directed by Harriet Gillies and produced by Blancmange Productions with The Rocks Village Bizarre.

Since 2017/2018 we have been working on the as-yet-unproduced *Seven Social Sins*, a theatrical response to the Reverend Frederick Lewis Donaldon's 'seven deadly social evils'.

We also blog, more or less regularly, at http://sevenon.blogspot.com.au

THE PLAYWRIGHTS

DONNA ABELA

Donna Abela's body of work includes plays which have won the Griffin Playwriting Prize and the AWGIE award for Stage (*Jump for Jordan*), AWGIE awards for radio (*Spirit, Aurora's Lament, Mrs Macquarie's Cello*), the Human Rights Award for Drama (*Highest Mountain Fastest River*), and been nominated for NSW Premiers Literary Awards (*Tales From the Arabian Night, Jump For Jordan*). For Kim Carpenter's Theatre of Image, she wrote two large scale adaptations: *Monkey ... Journey to the West* (2014 Brisbane Festival, 2015 Melbourne Festival, 2015 Sydney Opera House program) and *Tales from the Arabian Nights*, a widely produced play on refugee themes which was published by Currency Press in 2019. Donna completed her doctorate at the University of Wollongong where she teaches in the creative writing program. She works extensively as a dramaturge, mentor, and teaching artist, and is a proud founding member of PYT Fairfield (formerly Powerhouse Youth Theatre).

VANESSA BATES

Vanessa Bates is an award-winning playwright (a 2012 NSW Premier's Literary Award and most recently the 2019 AWGIE Award for Theatre for Young Audiences). Her plays include *A Ghost In My Suitcase (the play), Trailer, Light Begins To Fade, Every Second, The Magic Hour, PORN.CAKE, Checklist For An Armed Robber, Chipper* and *Darling Oscar*. Currently under commission with Sydney's Ensemble Theatre to write *The One*, Vanessa's work has been produced at Malthouse Theatre, Barking Gecko, Sydney Theatre Company, Darlinghurst Theatre, Black Swan Theatre, Griffin, Deckchair, Theatre@Risk, atyp, Tantrum and many others. A graduate of the NIDA Playwrights' Studio, Vanessa is also a playwriting teacher, running workshops for schools, theatre and writers' festivals. Currency Press have published several of Vanessa's plays including *A Ghost In My Suitcase*, *Trailer* and *Checklist For An Armed Robber*.

HILARY BELL

Hilary Bell's plays have been produced nationally by Griffin, Sydney Theatre Company, Black Swan, the Sydney Opera House, Arts Centre Melbourne, Deckchair, La Boite, State Theatre Company of South Australia, NORPA, Darlinghurst Theatre Company, City Recital Hall, National Theatre of Parramatta, the Ensemble and Vitalstatistix; in the US by Atlantic and Steppenwolf; in the UK by the National Theatre. They include *Wolf Lullaby, The Bloody Bride, Perfect Stranger, Memmie Le Blanc, The Red Balloon, The White Divers of Broome, Splinter, Victim Sidekick Boyfriend Me, The Red Tree,* and adaptations of *The Seagull, The Comedy of Errors, A Christmas Carol* and *The Hypochondriac*. She also writes libretti for opera, musicals and song cycles. Hilary is co-creator of several picture books including bestseller 'Alphabetical Sydney' with Antonia Pesenti. She is a graduate of the Juilliard Playwrights' Program, NIDA and AFTRS, and was the Tennessee Williams Fellow 2003-04 and the 2012 Patrick White Playwrights Fellow. Awards include a Helpmann, two AWGIES, the Jill Blewitt, an Inscription and the inaugural Philip Parsons Award.

https://hilarybell.org/

NOËLLE JANACZEWSKA

Noëlle Janaczewska is a playwright, poet, essayist and the author of *The Book of Thistles* (UWA Publishing)—part environmental history, part poetry, part unconventional memoir. She is the recipient of multiple awards, fellowships and residencies, including the 2020 NSW Premier's Digital History Prize, a Queensland Premier's Literary Award, the Griffin Award, ten AWGIE (Australian Writers' Guild Industry Excellence) Awards and a Windham-Campbell Prize from Yale University for her body of work as a dramatist. Noëlle's

recent productions and publications include: *Experiment Street* (ABC Radio National, 2019); *Yellow Yellow Sometimes Blue* (Q Theatre /Joan Sutherland Performing Arts Centre, Sydney, 2018); *Seoul City Sue* (ABC Radio National, 2018); audio scripts for the National Museum of Australia and the British Museum's 'Rome: City and Empire' exhibition, and *Good With Maps* (Siren Theatre Company, multiple seasons 2016–2021). Noëlle's latest book is *Scratchland* (UWA Publishing Poetry Series, 2020).
https://noelle-janaczewska
https://eatthetable.com

VERITY LAUGHTON

Verity Laughton is an award-winning Adelaide-based poet and playwright. Her work has been produced nationally and internationally. Her most recent productions are the verbatim theatre piece *Long Tan*, (April 2017) and the document-sourced *The Red Cross Letters*, (August 2016). Awards include AWGIES for Radio Drama and Community, the Inscription Open Award and the Griffin Award. Nominations include Griffin Theatre's Martin Lysicrates Prize, the STC Patrick White Award, the Bruce Dawe Poetry Prize, the Rodney Seaborne Prize (twice), the Blake Poetry Prize, the New Dramatists' Award, and the SA Critics' Circle Best New Play Award. She has recently completed a PhD in political theatre at Flinders University. The theatre project for the doctorate, about the post-World War 2 Polish diaspora, is entitled, *Bloodlines: A Polish Memory*.
https://www.veritylaughton.com

NED MANNING

Ned Manning is a writer, actor and teacher. His published plays include *Us or Them*, *Milo*, *Close to the Bone*, *Luck of the Draw*, *Kenny's Coming Home* (Currency Press) and *Alice Dreaming* (Cambridge University Press). *Alice Dreaming* has had over 20 productions by youth groups and schools, the latest being at Newcastle's Young People's Theatre (November 2021). His adaptation of *Women of Troy* (ABC Radio) was selected for competition in the Prix Marulic, Croatia's International

Festival for radio drama. Ned has written 10 plays for schools under the title, *Shakespeare for Australian Schools* (available at apt.org.au) that were originally developed for Bell Shakespeare's Actors at Work program. *Romeo & Juliet Intensive* was nominated for an AWGIE. His latest play, *Tsunami*, was shortlisted for the Patrick White Award. Ned's work of non-fiction, *Playground Duty* (New South Books) is a celebration of the teaching profession and a 'survival guide' for young teachers. As an actor Ned has appeared in many Australian productions, including the cult hit, *Dead End Drive-In*. He is currently working on his first novel.

https://www.nedmanning.com

CATHERINE ZIMDAHL

Catherine Zimdahl is playwright, screenwriter and visual artist. Her plays include *Step Up Stare Down*, *Deviant Art for the Degenerate*, *A Day Too Great*, *HereNowThenThere*, *Clark in Sarajevo*, *Family Running for Mr Whippy*, *Left Breathless a Question*, *The Fox*, *A World into A Child, A Child into the World* and *Moonfleet*. Catherine's works have been produced around Australia by the Sydney Theatre Company, Melbourne Theatre Company, the Griffin Theatre Company, Windmill National Children's Theatre and ABC Radio, amongst others. Awards include Griffin Playwriting Award, Victorian Premier's Literary Award, New Dramatists Exchange and AACTA Awards for Best Short Film and Best Screenplay. Catherine studied screenwriting at the Australian, Film, Television and Radio School where she was the recipient of the Qantas Travel Award graduate prize. Her feature film script *The Ego Trip* is currently in development and her most recent play *Gifted* received dramaturgical and workshop support through Playwriting Australia's Duologue Program.

https://catherine-zimdahl.squarespace.com/
https://www.instagram.com/zimdahlartspecies/

www.currency.com.au

Visit Currency Press' website now to:

- Buy your books online
- Browse through our full list of titles, from plays to screenplays, books on theatre, film and music, and more
- Choose a play for your school or amateur performance group by cast size and gender
- Obtain information about performance rights
- Find out about theatre productions and other performing arts news across Australia
- For students, read our study guides
- For teachers, access syllabus and other relevant information
- Sign up for our email newsletter

The performing arts publisher

www.ingramcontent.com/pod-product-compliance
Lightning Source LLC
Chambersburg PA
CBHW042130160426
43198CB00022B/2965